A Populist Challenge
to Corporate Capitalism

A Populist Challenge
to Corporate Capitalism

William Van Lear

Department of Economics, Belmont Abbey College

World Scientific
New Jersey • London • Singapore • Hong Kong

Published by

World Scientific Publishing Co. Pte. Ltd.

P O Box 128, Farrer Road, Singapore 912805

USA office: Suite 1B, 1060 Main Street, River Edge, NJ 07661

UK office: 57 Shelton Street, Covent Garden, London WC2H 9HE

British Library Cataloguing-in-Publication Data
A catalogue record for this book is available from the British Library.

A POPULIST CHALLENGE TO CORPORATE CAPITALISM

ISBN 981-02-4828-8

HB
51
.V33
2002

Printed in Singapore by Uto-Print

Contents

Contents

Acknowledgements

This book owes much to the life-long commitment of my wife to my success and happiness. Her general support and encouragement have helped me to excel in my profession and her specific assistance in improving my writing skills is appreciated.

Marietta College political science professor Michael Tager and Belmont Abbey College sociology professor Gary Williams were instrumental in bringing coherence to my project and made helpful suggestions on improving the content of the text. A number of my colleagues in the Humanities and Social Science divisions of the college have been helpful to me over the years in enlarging my perspective and bringing me in contact with a wide array of books and ideas. My students have also challenged my thinking and understanding of issues, and therefore have contributed to the ideas in the book.

Two prominent twentieth century economists and a modern writer on American history and politics have influenced my thinking. John M. Keynes' important work on macroeconomic dynamics provides a rich and insightful account on how the economy works. John K. Galbraith has been instrumental in integrating politics with economics, and has made insightful commentary on issues of power, income distribution, and conflict. Michael Lind's work in the 1990s explains the political-economic shifts in modern America. All of these authors have a sense of history, and employ analysis grounded in institutions and class conflict. Their work has social importance and is humanistic. Their efforts inspire me and I model my work on their contributions.

Many thanks go to family member Jeff MacConnell for provoking my thinking and challenging my beliefs about the economy and society. Debra Heath, information technologist at Belmont Abbey College, and Sooran Sundaresan of World Scientific Publishing Company, provided very helpful technical assistance.

Chapter 1

Introduction

The purpose of this book is to identify some important developments in the evolution of capitalism and to judge whether this evolution is in accord with fundamental American principles. Particular attention is paid to corporate governance, the investment-finance link in the economy, and monetary issues. The corporation has been the dominant enterprise in the American economy for some time and much more recently, money manager capitalism has altered capitalist finance and corporate governance. Is the corporation and money manager capitalism congruent with basic foundational principles of American society? Public policy should be grounded in American values, and this book will examine whether contemporary monetary policy is compatible with American principles and current economic evolution. It is argued that populist values inform the American republic. These are the central questions and issues that frame this book.

To give a proper context for understanding the book's central questions, I first explore the issue of income distribution. All societies must determine how rights to property and income are to be allocated. Different societies throughout history have employed different institutions or means to distribute income and wealth, and often income allocation and inequality have prompted criticism and conflict. United States income data are reviewed. Despite the general American acceptance of inequality, an inequality based on merit and productivity differences, the actual inequalities of our society are extreme and are not acceptable by American standards. This chapter explains income distribution, why we should care how income is distributed, and the prevalent myths that justify great inequalities.

1

Next, I layout the economic context that is crucial to creating a positive or negative environment from which business is conducted. Business investment drives innovation and economic growth, and depends heavily on profit income to motivate risk taking and as provision for finance. But investment drives profit as well because business spending on capital goods and production inputs determines income for the firms selling the capital and inputs. Government policy and regulation, Federal Reserve interest rate policy, and the social-economic setting create the backdrop for business investment and macroeconomic performance. Capitalist economies are dynamic with a penchant for expansion and innovation but growth does not move along an uninterrupted straight line. Business cycles and financial crises are inherent features of capitalist societies, and they affect and are affected by the prevailing economic climate. The existing income distribution can influence the vitality of an economy and the degree to which there is popular acceptance of the system. The text explains the great 1990s expansion and why it may end.

The American economy has evolved through a series of distinct stages. This book takes the reader chronologically through these stages, identifying the distinguishing characteristics of each epoch. Focus is placed on specific institutional features. What most concerns me is the governance system of business, and the means by which firms raise capital to finance investment. Who has power in the firm, and over finance, matters for the macroeconomic functioning of the economy. Business cycles, growth, and the economic environment are all affected by the particular stage in force.

Important recent developments in economic structure are identified, of which great attention is given to the description and importance of money manager capitalism. Large pension and mutual funds have surpassed banks as leading financial institutions, and money managers are important in affecting the flow of funds and financial asset prices of the economy's major corporations. An argument is made that this change in finance has significant macroeconomic implications and the book provides some empirical evidence to buttress that case. Furthermore, there is a particular monetary policy regime associated with the current economic stage. Policy has returned to a

Classical orientation,[1] quite consistent with much of monetary policy history in the United States. The book explains the conventional wisdom of how monetary policy works and provides an historical overview of the history of policy. The heterodox economic view is then contrasted with the conventional perspective of monetary policy, and it is argued that business should accept the responsibility of controlling inflation. Reforming monetary policy along heterodox lines is consistent with the current stage of money manager capitalism, whereas the current Classical orientation is incompatible.

The subsequent section of the text presents the central argument. America is based on a set of core principles, as laid out by important documents, thinkers, and eras. These principles inform American political economy and are populist oriented. Yet, despite explicit foundational principles, U.S. economic history demonstrates that the central business unit, namely the corporation, has evolved along a path inconsistent with these principles. American populism of the late nineteenth century attempted to restructure the country back along its intended path but failed. This book calls for a renewal of populist economic reform, and describes what contemporary forces may pull America along such a path. In particular, the corporation may be pressured over the long run to change in ways more compatible with America's roots.

The final section of the text summarizes the main points of the earlier chapters and revisits the topic of economic booms. Eight populist policy reforms are suggested that could create a modicum of success in the short run at redirecting American economic life. The book ends with further reflections on democracy and politics.

In sum, this book is a discourse in political economy and is instructional in that it describes the causes of economic growth and cycles, and the

---

[1] The Classical Tradition in monetary policy is based on what economists call the quantity theory of money. This notion argues that the government or central bank controls the quantity and growth of the money supply in an economy. Money growth affects only the price level and not employment and production in the economy. Limiting money growth creates price stability and stabilizes economic activity according to this view.

process by which monetary policy affects economic activity. This effort pulls together elements of American history and important political-economic concepts to argue that contemporary monetary policy and the corporate form of business are not consistent with either money manager capitalism or the country's founding principles. The book conveys an appreciation for institutional and policy evolution, and undertakes a critical examination of the current stage of economic development. And finally, the work draws a sharp distinction between America's populist foundational values and the prevailing dominant values of the U.S. elite.

Chapter 2

Wealth and Income Distribution

Capitalism coexists uneasily with its income distribution. Low income and little wealth accumulation by some exist simultaneously with the attainment of ultra high income and wealth of others. Unrest occasionally breaks out over the allocation of capitalism's economic pie. The substantial concentration of income that prevails provokes interest into the causes of such concentration. Great inequalities affect the economy and politics, and such stratified societies require the use of myths to justify inequality. Precedent is set for concern over inequality, as a long line of scholars has considered the subject.[1]

Let's begin by demonstrating that meaningful income and wealth disparities exist.

Income and Wealth Distribution Data

Many studies conducted over the 1980s and 1990s confirm an increase in income and wealth inequality. The shares of net wealth and net financial wealth commanded by the top 20% and bottom 40% are revealing. The top 20% of wealth holders' net wealth, or assets minus liabilities, increased from about 81% in the early 1980s to 84% in the mid 1990s, while their net financial wealth increased from 91% to 93%. Financial wealth only measures financial assets and liabilities. The bottom 40% have significantly lower

---

[1] Aristotle, Rousseau, Marx, Mill, Tocqueville, Tawney, and Rawls are prominent figures who have addressed the issue of inequality. Recent work by economists such as Milton Friedman [1980] and Lester Thurow [1985, 1996], and legal scholar Lawrence Mitchell [1998] are noteworthy.

numbers. Net wealth over this time period is less than 1%, and net financial wealth ranges between negative .9% to negative 2.4%. The share of wealth held by the top 1% of households increased from 25% in 1980 to 36% in 1990 to 40% in 1997 [USNews 2/21/00, p42]. Median net worth of Americans was $60,700 in 1998 [BW 7/31/00, p34]. A look at the composition of wealth demonstrates that these wealth classes own assets in different proportions. The bottom 80% of households have 66% of their wealth in primary real estate and another 5% in other real estate. The top 1% of households have 67% of their assets in business equity and financial assets.

Surprisingly, as the fraction of Americans owning bonds and stocks has increased, the concentration of financial asset ownership has also increased. Using Federal Reserve data, one study reports that the share of total household net wealth held by the top 1% rose from 30.1% in 1992 to an even 34% in 1998, while the share of the bottom 90% fell from 33% to 31.3% over the same period [BW 6/19/00, p38]. American median net wealth and stock ownership is up markedly in the 1990s, but the relative position of most people had fallen.

Note in the table below that stock ownership is concentrated among high-income earners and that the top 16.2% of households control 74.7% of all stock.

Concentration of Stock Ownership by Income Class, 1998					
	Percentage of Households Owning Stock Worth More Than			Percentage of Stock Owned	
Income Level	Share of Households	Zero	$4,999	$9,999	Shares	Cumulative
$250,000 or more	1.6	93.3	92.7	91.9	36.1	36.1
$100,000–$249,999	6.9	89.0	85.5	82.8	27.7	63.9
$75,000–$99,999	7.7	80.7	70.4	66.5	10.8	74.7
$50,000–$74,999	17.4	70.9	55.6	48.8	13.1	87.8
$25,000–$49,999	29.0	52.0	34.3	27.4	8.5	96.3
$15,000–$24,999	16.1	29.2	16.9	12.9	2.6	98.9
Under $15,000	21.3	0.6	5.2	4.5	1.1	100.0
All	100.0	48.2	36.3	31.8	100.0	

Note: Includes direct ownership of stock and indirect ownership through mutual funds, trusts, IRAs, Keogh plans, 401(k) plans, and other retirement accounts.

Source: Edward Wolff. "The Rich Get Richer..." Levy Economics Institute, Spring 2001, p.6.

Another telling statistic is the growth in annual family income by income group, comparing the 1947–1973 period with modern times of 1973–1996. In the early period, income growth was well above 2% for all income groups, with middle and lower income groups receiving the highest growth. And income growth across income groups was distributed very evenly. But in the latter period, growth rates fall markedly, never exceeding 1.3% per year. The growth rate for the bottom 60% was negative. The growth in income for the bottom 80% was lower than for the top 20%. And finally, the distribution of growth was much more uneven, with slightly higher rates achieved by each successively higher income group.

Looking at the ratio of income of the top to bottom 20%, and the real pre-tax income growth of the top to bottom 20%, further demonstrates a growing income dispersion. In the late 1970s, the income ratio was 7.4 but by the late 1990s the ratio increased to 10.6. Real income growth over the last ten years, in 1997 dollars, was $17,800 for the top 20%, but only $100 for the bottom 20% [BW 1/31/00, p34]. The ratio of CEO pay to non-management worker pay has risen markedly since the 1970s. In the 1970s the ratio stood at 40 to 1. By 1990, the ratio advanced to about 100 to 1 and in 1998 was about 450 to 1 [USNews 2/21/00, p42].

Inequality within the working class has grown as well. Incomes of white-collar professionals and people with college degrees have increased more rapidly than the incomes of other types of workers. This twenty-year trend is documented by Reich [1992] and Palley [2001]. Palley reports that an income shift away from non-supervisory labor, who make-up 80% of the workforce, towards managerial workers has raised family income inequality. While income has shifted towards white collar labor, lower income households are burden by higher debt to income ratios [2, 6].

Understanding Capitalist Income Distribution

What are the root causes of great income inequities in the U.S.? The following discussion offers an explanation.

Two basic kinds of income prevail, labor and property income. Labor income is paid in the form of wages, salaries, and benefits, and is earned in the employ of others. Labor income varies across jobs and professions ranging from just a few thousand dollars per year to the low six figures. Within job categories, relatively narrow ranges of pay prevail and most people's earnings are not under their control. Most workers have no other means to support themselves except by selling their skills and effort to employers, and labor works at the convenience and pleasure of employers. Labor incomes depend on the sales and profits of the firms they work for and how productive they are believed to be by employers. Conversely, property income consists of earnings from rent, interest, profit, and capital gain. This income is quite variable and open- ended in that large losses or gains can be had. Property income is derived from commerce, finance, speculation on and trading of commodities or property, and mergers and acquisitions of enterprises. Property income depends principally on the accumulation of capital and people under control by the owners and executives of enterprise. Hence income levels and distribution have much to do with one's function, and what one owns, in the economy. What matters most for distribution is whether one labors for another or is engaged in the control of property and people.

Incomes earned depend importantly on people's function within economic organizations and their role in the direction or management of organizations. Administrative work is often so well compensated that their income is not proportioned to others whom they work with or supervise. Administration of strategic planning, budgeting, finance, marketing, and innovation in firms entails substantial responsibility and power to effect change. With position of great responsibility and power comes concomitant pecuniary reward. Positions that are enhanced by status or prestige receive even greater compensation. Thus income levels and distribution are very much the result of one's position in an economic hierarchy and the value placed on those positions. Note the high status and incomes of the executive class. Moreover, American society has an exaggerated notion of the importance or contribution of the individual. Though most individuals work in organizations, whose accomplishments require substantial cooperation with people in and among institutions, a few particular individuals are typically singled out as responsible for whatever is accomplished. Their incomes and status are consequently elevated. And further, these elites tend to be a self perpetuating interlocking group who are responsible for hiring and paying each other as they sit on company boards and contribute to trade associations, lobbies, and think tanks. Opportunities for prominence are created in the performance of high-level government work and political campaigns.

Economic wellbeing is often associated with group effort and connections. Economic development is typically pursued by cliques which assemble complementary business, legal, and financial acumen. Successful projects usually require a variety of skills and knowledge that can only be achieved through concerted group action. Opportunities, perceived or created, and how opportunities are distributed, profoundly impact economic success. Income dispersion is the effect of varying social-economic connections and the degree to which business cliques are difficult to penetrate or form. Sufficient opportunities, good contacts, and networking are essential to high financial remuneration. But for most Americans, social/economic circumstances limit the range of viable opportunities. Effective use of connections requires that personal contacts be of some prominence and necessitates particular social skills and personalities suitable for penetrating cliques of people with egos and influence. Moreover, substantial inheritances facilitate business formation or expansion, and provide the means to purchase important connections and create networks. In fact, inherited wealth tends to attract financial capital and business acumen. Given the substantial wealth concentration in the U.S., intergenerational transfers of property and money give enormous economic advantages to a marked few.

Certainly, one of the most distinguishing attributes of capitalism is the employer-employee relationship. The far majority of people work for someone else. Compensation, the work day, and working conditions, the location and permanence of the work, and decisions as to the technology employed and amount of investment are, for the most part, determined by the ten percent of the population who are employers and property owners. Labor and technology are productively employed through business organizations where the most dominant is the corporation. The source of property income is labor, and therefore the more command one has over labor, the higher the property income. Hence the incessant and even habitual drive to integrate businesses under small numbers of vested interests.

The common institutional link among the factors responsible for great income disparities is the corporation. The legal creation known as the corporation is an economic accumulation device, effective in acquiring, organizing, and employing large amounts of capital and people, to produce and distribute goods and services. Executives and stockholders who run the corporations can magnify their incomes by assembling ever-larger enterprises employing more people and capital. Opportunities and connections are best exploited from within the corporate structure, and the success of corporate business has brought high praise and status to its controllers. While large numbers of people are actually responsible for production and sales, the distribution of income within corporations is determined by its controllers. And therefore, the principal reason for the existence of large income inequalities is the existence of the corporation.[2]

Why Care About Inequality?

Why care that the income distribution is so highly concentrated in society? What specifically are the consequences of great inequality?

First there are certain economic considerations. When a small percentage of people receive a large fraction of national income, these relatively few people enjoy disproportionately the material fruits of economic progress. The amenities and comforts of life are consumed by the few, though produced by the many. Consumer luxuries, the best education, full access to health care, and greater leisure are afforded to the affluent. Fewer pleasures, lower quality goods and services, and generally poorer material surroundings are what the less fortunate experience. Inheritances are passed down to children and grand children who do not work for a living, yet have the power to significantly influence business and politics.

---

[2] This chapter discusses the most basic factors affecting inequality. But this is not to suggest that public policies play no role. They do. Policies promoting globalization, welfare changes, tax reforms, etc. all affect what people earn. Monetary policy's influence on distribution is discussed in chapter seven.

And society's macroeconomic environment is affected. The amassing of wealth increases the savings and speculative proclivity of the country's affluent and others attempting to copy the performance of the successful. Speculation can produce financial and commercial instability, as funds are allocated towards trading in financial assets and currency. Price declines in these assets negatively affect business optimism and job-enhancing investment. Excessive preference for trading and saving reduces economic vitality by lessening business commitment to long run economic development.

National growth rates can slow markedly or the economy may stagnate from much inequality. As incomes become concentrated, the percentage of savings to national income rises as the well off have more or less fulfilled their consumption goals. Money is diverted to speculation and/or the purchase of financial assets and real estate. Less money reenters the economy, via the household consumption-business investment route, which reduces commercial sales and profits. As spending slows, so do profits and the incentive to grow employment and production. Eventually unemployment increases as labor force growth exceeds hiring. Stagnation or recession sets in.

The famous macroeconomist John Maynard Keynes attacked the notion that the savings of the wealthy are needed for growth. In his policy chapter which concludes his important economic treatise *The General Theory*, he writes:

> ... up to the point where full employment prevails, the growth of capital depends not at all on a low propensity to consume but is, on the contrary, held back by it; and only in conditions of full employment is a low propensity to consume conducive to the growth of capital. Moreover, experience suggests that in existing conditions saving ... is more than adequate, and that measures for the redistribution of incomes in a way likely to raise the propensity to consume may prove positively favorable to the growth of capital.[3]

---

[3] See Keynes [1964] chapter 24, and in particular pages 372 to 373.

Social conflict and upheaval can result from great income disparities. While wealth distribution is rarely a topic of public discourse, economic difficulties and particularly economic contraction can focus attention on distributive issues. Rising national income is usually distributed sufficiently broadly to appease most people during growth periods. Yet prodigious incomes or a disproportionate share of income increases going to the few, publicized to the many, bring consternation. Questions of fairness and distributive justice come to the forefront. The basic goodness of a society is questioned when income-gains accrue to a small percentage of people, generating a sense that privilege prevails. And when recessions and stagnation accompany inequality, economic difficulties intensify public discussion and discontent over distributional aspects of private and public policies.

Whether or not inequality becomes a political issue, economic power translates into political power. Politicians and parties cater to and are moved by centers of wealth. In fact the whole political debate during campaigns will tend to identify only a narrow set of problems as issues, typically those problems most important to the affluent or business or Wall Street. A genuine competitive politics requires a full airing of issues and perspectives, but a polity dominated by economic elites circumscribes public discussion, narrows the choice of politicians, leads to a corporate dominated media, reduces public political participation, and fosters political alienation and cynicism.

A final important effect of great inequality is that the tastes and needs of the affluent are most serviced relative to lower income consumers. Business responds to profits and those with the greatest purchasing power drive sales. Those with the most to spend buy goods and services that have the highest returns for entrepreneurs. Luxury and large cars, large homes, extravagant vacations, all earn business high profits. Research and resources flow to where the highest returns are being made. Advertising and sales efforts create and reinforce the purchase and production of relatively expensive and high return items. Wealthy consumers move business and business develops new products based on expectations of higher than normal returns by catering to affluency. The modern drive to enhance service, and garner a competitive edge based on service, is a consequence of the growing inequality in contemporary America.

The Importance of Myth

Myth plays an important function. Mythical ideas and theories tend to obscure reality and justify inequality. Arguments with much falsity are actually quite effective if they contain an element of truth. It is this element that makes them appealing.

The idea that the Federal Reserve is a public policymaking body obscures reality and justifies inequality. Despite Fed pronouncements and business journalism reporting, the American central bank is importantly influenced on the Board by conservatively minded public appointees and banker representatives on the all-important Federal Open Market Committee, the policymaking arm of the Bank. Commercial bank influence is directed through the Federal Advisory Committee and Wall Street impact is expressed through the bond market, which Fed officials watch for clues as to how interest rates should move. The preferred monetary policy is to restrict bank liquidity to keep the value of money high as measured by significantly positive borrowing costs and price stability. This policy augments creditor incomes and loan portfolios, benefiting principally the affluent, at the expense of most Americans and small firms that do most of the borrowing. Such policies also tend to limit employment and profit opportunities, and prevent a broad distribution of the economy's earnings, in order to curtail inflation. Obfuscation presents the central bank as public spirited, and income inequality favoring wealthy financiers is justified in the name of promoting economic stability and encouraging risktaking.

The economic system is not structured to allow the many to become wealthy, whatever they do. The accepted dictum is that Americans of every class should simply follow the economic behavior of wealthy people; mimicking the virtue of consistent and disciplined saving, complemented by compounding, will make virtually any portfolio grow into millions of dollars. While possible for some, such finance, if practiced by even twenty percent of the population, would lead to macroeconomic collapse. The economy is not driven by saving and production as the myth contends but by money creation and spending. It's the latter that promotes sales and profits that in turn determine financial asset values. If the bulk of the population reduced spending to save more, stock and bond prices would plummet as profits fell. Not only would the wealthy not be wealthy, but the employer class would layoff many of those who committed themselves to emulating the virtuous affluent. The financial success of the few obscures the reality of how capitalist finance works for the whole. The resulting inequality is justified by attribution of success to the risk-taking and intelligence of superior people.

Another myth is that efficiency imperatives drive firms to become big. It is said that firms must grow very large to reap economies of scale. Some companies can indeed increase efficiency by enlarging operations. Certain technological improvements are applicable to the manufacture of particular goods, automobiles as an example, that enable firms to produce at lower average cost as they acquire a larger share of the market. But firms exploit the public's misunderstanding of the matter. Economies of scale are relevant to the proper size of individual plants, not entire companies. Every given plant should be of adequate size to minimize unit costs, and therefore firms need to be of that size to be efficient. But in no way does efficiency require that ownership and control be held in common over many plants of efficient size. Yet this is exactly what constitutes modern corporate business and explains why a few people are so wealthy. Nevertheless, the efficiency myth justifies ultra-large enterprises and great income disparities. Mergers beget big business, and big incomes are the reward for accumulation not efficiency.

A final example of myth affecting income distribution comes from the notion of "Economic Naturalism." Economic Naturalism is an idea advocated by contemporary conservative thinkers. It argues that economic conditions and outcomes result from individual initiative and action. And it's nature that informs people; capitalism is a natural system and is an expression of free persons engaged in a competitive dynamic driven by self-interest. What is natural is "good and right". This notion is a great over-simplification of reality of course. No system or set of institutions is natural; systems arise from human design and are open to modification. The concept of naturalism justifies any income distribution, and excuses its proponents from any responsibility to address or defend the current economic allocation. Equating any economy with nature tends to shield the system from culpability for any outcome.

Moreover, economic events and outcomes result from more than individual initiative. Policy and institutions are of paramount importance. If the Central Bank establishes a high interest rate regime, wealthy Americans benefit because they are the creditors to the economy. But the Federal Reserve could establish and justify a low rate regime, favoring debtors and low-income people. And the impetus to economic activity is largely accomplished through institutions such as corporations and Wall Street. These institutions are the composite of group interaction and cooperation, informed by a common value set. Large enterprises are the result of, over a long time frame, competition, technology, and mergers. Their impact greatly exceeds that of individuals and for the most part supplants individual effort. Income distribution is affected by institutional decisions and the relative power of institutions, and is not merely the outcome of individual accomplishment.

Final Comments

It's clearly apparent that many economists and politicians accept or do not care about large income and wealth inequalities. Notice the minimal attention paid to inequality during political campaigns. Notice the more frequent desire to cut progressive taxes and ignore or raise regressive taxes. Note the great resistance to imposing price ceilings or limitations on the oil and drug industries, or interest rate caps on banking. Others recognize the inequality issue but argue that inequality is justified and functional or that particular social facts mitigate any strong remedial public policy compulsion.[4]

Inequality is justified as the expectant outcome of unequal and competitive people. It is functional supposedly because it creates incentives to get ahead. And a vexing conscience is comforted by knowing that great upward mobility avails itself to the hard working and sacrificing American. Anyhow, no arbitrary obstacles are in place that could keep deserving people from obtaining financial success. And price controls and progressive taxes create far greater problems than those that stem from inequality.

---

[4] Such social "facts" are that the poor deserve their condition for various personal failings and decisions.

What's striking is the selective use of argument concerning inequality by pundits. For some, any degree of inequality is justified due to natural differences in ability or motivation. Any attempt to moderate the extremes is viewed as unacceptable social engineering. Yet when inequality-enhancing economic policies enter public discussion, argument is reframed. Instead of focusing on the supposed deleterious effects of policy intervention, emphasis shifts to how *Americans* stand to gain from these policies. In fact, a policy-induced increase in income concentration is said to prompt private interest to meet social need through more investment. Implicit in this reasoning is that affluent beneficiaries of public policy are not different in any meaningful way from most Americans. We all are now somehow equal and thus equally deserving of government largess irrespective of class. Upper class people have all the same worries and responsibilities as everyone else. How base to view America as class structured and stratified![5]

Inequality can impede the resolution of other problems by limiting the possible solutions to those problems. Take inflation for example. Substantial inequality and inflation contribute to episodic crises. For instance, rising prices for health care and energy, in a society of great inequality, create dissatisfaction among the public and problems for politicians. Inflation in industry prices of essential goods is partly responsible for the large incomes of some, while great income inequality makes it difficult for low and modest income earners to afford these goods. Much attention is then directed towards resolving these kind of crises, often by government subsidizing the cost for consumers, not by addressing the core of the problem, namely the inflation of incomes of those whose incomes far exceed what most people make. Price controls and/or increasing tax progressivity are ruled out categorically,

---

[5] Congressional tax debates of Summer 2000 exemplify this. Conservatives were arguing that eliminating the estate tax helps small farmers and business people, and that it is immoral to tax some American differently than others. But the facts of the estate tax are that very few small enterprises are ever touched by the tax and the tax's purpose is to prevent a trust fund leisure class from developing.

and do not enter public debate or consideration.[6]

But of course great inequality must somehow be legitimated. Myths have a role and some were discussed at an earlier point in this chapter. The notion of "just rewards" is well received in the United States and most people believe that opportunities exist for advancement. Yet again most Americans know that while many occupational paths are possibilities, attainment of high income is strictly limited and large income differentials result from more than differences in skills and motivations. Nevertheless, broad support, or at least acquiescence, exists for our competitive stratified society. And it is not just myth or ignorance or bamboozlement that explains this acceptance. Capitalism produces concrete evidence of success: growth, innovation, progress, material comforts. There is political democracy and civil liberties, and people have certain rights and protections. What makes an assault on vast inequalities difficult is that reformers have to convince people to care about inequality when there is usually no concrete and recognizable life experience basis for much concern.[7]

Income distribution has a relevancy to the remainder of the text. Substantial inequality, as already argued, heightens the degree of speculation in financial markets and can undermine economic growth. But income distribution also has a bearing on financial crises and business cycles, a matter discussed in the next chapter. In particular, the distribution of profit to wages affects the inclination to invest and the vitality of an economy. Furthermore, specific eras of Capitalism can be identified where there was a shift toward greater or lower equality. This text marks out these periods.

---

[6] Consider the California energy issue of 2000–2001. The governor wanted price caps on energy costs that had increased 400% over a matter of months. Classical economists objected, arguing that such a policy distorts efficient markets and that the higher profits would finance an augmentation in the state's energy production capacity. This position represents Classical support for inflation. Evidently, inflation in one or related industries is actually socially beneficial. Yet when the same economists measure price increases across many industries to compute aggregate inflation, they strongly support central bank restrictive policies to combat this inflation. Aggregate inflation is socially detrimental while single-industry inflation has a warranted public purpose.

[7] Sociologists have done much work on stratification and legitimization. See the work of Kerbo (1991) for a complete discussion.

Our modern era has promoted increased inequality. Besides the influence of private sector developments on wealth distribution, public policy effects are important as well, and the role of monetary policy will be of central focus in chapter six. And finally, there is an American conception of equality that has shaped American society, and this ideal plays some importance in the argument conveyed in chapter seven.

Epilogue on Incentives

Conventional wisdom has it that people require significant financial inducement to compel labor. When economic performance deteriorates, conventional thinkers quickly advocate public policy measures to improve or restore incentives to resuscitate growth. Somehow the incentives that were in place in the recent past, those responsible for fostering initiative and risk-taking during the boom, are undercut or weakened. The now in vogue Supply-Side theory of macroeconomics calls for upper class oriented tax cuts, regulatory reform, and other measures to stimulate productivity.

It is correct that incentives are fundamental to capitalist economics, but in the U.S. they have been in place since the beginning of the Republic. Legal and policy changes have occurred over time as circumstances have changed, but the foundation creating entrepreneurial incentives and hard work has always been with us. What brings on recession and economic decline are developments internal to capitalism's operations, not a deterioration in basic incentives. And acceptance of conventional wisdom has a very negative implication for America's income distribution over the long run. As this chapter demonstrates, distributional shifts since the 1970s have favored the well to do, and to some extent, at the expense of others. If public policy were to apply Supply-Side theory every time growth slows, which can occur two or three times a decade, that policy would induce further income inequality throughout society. Despite recent vast increases in income to and policies favorable to the wealthy, are we to believe that inadequate incentives are responsible for the current economic slowdown?

Chapter 3

Growth, Cycles, And Crises

The prime task of this chapter is to describe and explain the basic nature of capitalism. A capitalist economy moves through cycles. It exhibits a continuous process of expansions and contractions in activity, modified each time by the prevailing institutions of the day and the public policy regime in force. Resurfacing throughout this discussion is the role of income distribution that affects and is affected by the economy's cycles and public policy.

Economic Growth

A vital, healthy, opportunity-generating economy comes from a background substantively different than a lackluster or contracting economy. A flourishing business sector for example, one with ample job and sales growth, requires that the prevailing economic environment be favorable to investment and profit. And a stable economic system necessitates the reproduction of institutions for long term development. Institutional evolution can send capitalism through successive waves of progress and decline.[1]

The business environment depends importantly in part on the investment opportunities that are available to or made by business, and business expectations about the profitability and risk of those investment opportunities. More investment is forthcoming when profitable opportunities abound, and entrepreneurs are optimistic about future returns. Business will prioritize

---

[1] See David Gordon's article "Up and Down the Long Roller Coaster," in the book U.S. Capitalism in Crisis, New York, Education Project of the Union for Radical Political Economics, 1978.

19

investments by their profitability and risk, selecting the highest yielding ones first for any given risk category.

Expectations critically affect lending and borrowing for investment. Creditors must assess the profitability and risk associated with any activity undertaken by a borrower. Lenders risk exists because of the uncertainty surrounding the debtor's ability and willingness to repay. Risk is added when bankers and bondholders have less knowledge about the borrower's project than the borrower does. Borrowers risk exists due to the guesswork involved in calculating revenues and expenses of long-term projects. And this risk is more subjective and non-contractual in nature than lenders risk.

Affecting lenders and businesses are speculative tendencies induced by the profit motive and competition. After economic expansions have persisted for some time, business and financiers tend to under-appreciate risk as success breeds confidence. Lending and borrowing are boosted. The combined effect of risk-taking and positive psychology propels economic activity and innovation.

If business opportunities expand along with confidence and optimism, corporate spending will increase, accommodated by bank lending. The increase in the capital stock and the money supply provide for more employment and income, generating the well-known multiplier effect. A positive multiplier effect arises from cumulative increases in spending financed by money creation. Increased employment and income produce further rounds of money creation through bank lending, thereby magnifying the impact of higher spending. Growth necessitates net deficit spending, meaning that those who are spending more than they are earning are more than offsetting those who are earning more than they are spending. The economy ascends to a higher GDP when deficit budgets exceed surplus budgets; only a net deficit financial position for the economy produces rising living standards. The following math example illustrates the point:

Macroeconomic equilibrium requires that spending be equal to income and GDP. Household consumption (C) plus business investment (I) plus government spending (G) plus foreign purchases of domestic goods or exports (X) must equal each sector's income, where Y stands for household income, P stands for business profits, T for taxes, and M for imports.

$$\text{Total Spending} = \text{Total Income} = \text{GDP}$$

$$C + I + G + X = Y + P + T + M = \text{GDP}$$

Subtracting each sector's income from its spending, and noting that total income equals GDP, we have

$$(C\text{-}Y) + (I\text{-}P) + (G\text{-}T) + (X\text{-}M) = \text{GDP} - \text{GDP} = 0$$

The above equation shows the budget position or financial balance of each sector when equilibrium exists. Growth occurs from one period to the next or from one equilibrium to the next, and is captured by the equation below:

$$d(C\text{-}Y) + d(I\text{-}P) + d(G\text{-}T) + d(X\text{-}M) = d(\text{GDP}),$$

where d means "change in".

For the economy to grow, which is for the change in GDP to be positive, money creation from bank lending must finance a net deficit budget stance. That is, from one period to the next, spending must be greater than income. As growth produces an equivalent amount of income, spending must rise further if growth is to continue. A no-growth economy is one where all sectors have balanced budgets or where any one sector's deficit is offset by surpluses elsewhere.

If investment opportunities decline and pessimism prevails, or risk-taking inclinations recede, investment falls, followed by a decline in employment, income, and bank lending. A negative multiplier is in play, manifested by a net surplus financial balance in the economy. Note as well that if any sector tries to save more by spending less, output contracts since spending determines income. The economy cannot save its way to growth.

Observe the paradoxical implication from the above analysis. Those who save to build wealth can only do so if others deficit spend, and it's the deficit spending that creates the opportunity to build wealth. While some individuals routinely save, our society as a whole cannot save. Saving in advance of borrowing would actually reduce the nation's wealth [J. Fagg Foster 1981]. Thus we can only conclude that the drivers of growth and wealth are workers and firms who deficit spend, often those whose living standards fall short of affluence. So therefore, great income inequality is not a necessity for prosperity but the result of property ownership concentration and corporatization as argued in the previous chapter.

Let's expand our consideration of important economic environmental factors. For instance, the environment depends on the policies of leading economic institutions in society. These policies affect the prevailing economic, political, and social conditions. For example, government policy sets tax rates and program priorities, and regulates commerce and banking. Monetary policy, conducted by the Treasury and Federal Reserve, sets interest rates, which in turn affect money growth and borrowing, exchange rates, and financial asset values. Monetary and fiscal policies influence the economy by altering private sector incomes, spending, and employment. Economic objectives are reflected in the budget priorities of government and in interest rate policy of the Federal Reserve.

Business policy is of paramount importance for determining economic performance. Business goals and decisions affect the level, pace, and direction of investment. Policy determines not only which technologies are developed and commercialized, but also the technologies themselves. It affects ownership relations among corporations, banks, and government, and how companies employ and relate to labor. And it affects the character and quality of community life and regional economic development. As such, this policy has a profound affect on macroeconomic conditions, reflected in employment and inflation rates, productivity and innovation, and ultimately growth and cycles.

Financial policy, coming from the leading securities firms, banks, mutual funds, and insurance companies, affects interest rates, financial asset prices, and exchange rates. The level, pace, and direction of business investment is influenced because this policy sets the cost and availability of credit. The financial sector affects investment through changes in corporate equity prices and dividend payouts, that influence financing costs and profitability, and through influence on corporate boards.[2]

---

[2] The role of financial crises and business cycles will be addressed below.

The development of both entrepreneurialism and finance, and the link between the two, affect economic growth. Business development spurs the demand for external finance and financial services. Financial sector development mobilizes savings and allocates savings to spending outlets. Finance takes the surpluses generated by some businesses and consumers and finds those who want to deficit spend. These two sectors tend to develop commensurately, development in each reinforcing and facilitating development in the other sector.[3] The Gurley-Shaw thesis states that nonbank financial institutions augment total private sector spending beyond what banks finance. These intermediaries offer higher returns and more financial services to clients, and therefore access and employ funds that would otherwise remain idle in banks, firms, or households. This increases the velocity of money not the quantity.[4]

The prevailing social conditions within society affect business investment. The prevailing gender, racial, and ethnic relationships, together with the extent of poverty and crime, impact work relationships and business costs. The political party and philosophy in power is important for its determination of public priority objectives, its capacity to serve social needs, and its commitment to economic growth. Other important aspects are the degree of public support for and existence of unions and labor rights enforcement, the status afforded to management and administration, and other established laws, conditions, or relationships critical to the distribution of income and power, property rights enforcement, encouragement of free enterprise, and the preservation of democracy and liberty.[5]

In an economy dominated by private investment and capital, a certain degree of income and political power concentration occurs over time in the business and financial community. Such concentration arises for several reasons. The constant pressures of competition over markets eventually leads to a few very successful enterprises and bankruptcies among the many. Changes in technology develop new markets to compete over and rearrange

---

[3] For a discussion of whether finance causes growth or not, see Khan [2000].

[4] See Gurley's and Shaw's text "Money in a Theory of Finance" [1960].

[5] The importance of these concepts is discussed in chapter seven.

who has a competitive edge. And the profit motive drives efforts to create new markets and gain competitive advantages. Again, only some firms will win the struggle and they ultimately become industry leaders. Concentration is furthered by government efforts that foster a pro-business investment and merger climate. Favorable tax treatment for property, secure legal protection for corporations, and measures to increase market size and share for big firms, such as free trade agreements or expansion of domestic demand, are the principal public policy means for providing not only profitable accumulation, but higher inequality.[6]

Business Cycles

Capitalist economies are inherently dynamic, subject to ebb and flow in activity. In the years prior to the 1940s, boom-bust cycles were the norm. Strong growth spurts were followed by collapses. Modern fiscal and monetary interventions by the state moderate cycle extremes but have not completely stabilized economic activity. The historical record shows an economy moving through cycles over time, marking out both short run fluctuations and longer run waves of expansions and contractions. Long run waves are propelled by marked changes in profitability driven by new kinds of technology and competition while short run cycles are driven mainly by short-term changes in business profitability.[7]

The best way to think about cycle generation is to understand that business profit and investment are interdependent and cyclical, and it's this relationship that produces cyclical economic activity. This profit-investment relationship operates in a circuit. In the first circuit, profit (P) is a function of investment (I). Here, investment drives business profits and promotes new industries and products, and new technologies, leading to increased demand and employment. Revenues rise as innovations are commercialized

---

[6] It will be argued in chapter six that Orthodox monetary policy promotes inequality because it favors returns to lenders, most of whom are affluent.

[7] The following is grounded in the work of Schumpeter [1942] and Kalecki [1971].

and costs fall from competition and efficiencies. Business profits increase consequently, thus affirming the Kaleckian notion that the business sector earns what firms invest. These profits are reinvested, paid to stockholders, or used to acquire other operations. A sustained period of expansion ensues. Circuit one looks as follows: $I \rightarrow P \rightarrow I$.

In circuit two, investment is a function of profit. Here, profits finance investment, and investment is undertaken to expand capacity or consolidate control over existing industries or technologies. Continued investment in established industries eventually squeezes profits as competition and market exploitation drive down earnings, and increased demand for credit raises financing costs. Circuit two affirms the notion that businesses spend what they earn. As earnings or earnings growth declines, firms spend less. This circuit is characterized by declining profitability and slowing growth. Circuit two is as follows: $P \rightarrow I \rightarrow P$.

Both circuits operate simultaneously but in different sectors or industries and one circuit can dominate in the economy for some period. Circuit one is noticeable during the recovery phase of economic activity, and is most pronounced during periods of substantial competition, market extension and economic transition. Increased income inequality and economic dislocation mark such eras. Some businesses and workers do exceedingly well because of increased opportunities for enterprise, while others suffer from an inability to adjust to competition or from a decrease in opportunities. This situation prompts conflict over income distribution within classes and across society. Circuit one dominated parts of the Robber Baron era of the late nineteenth century, the 1920s, the 1950s and 1960s, and most recently, the 1990s. The stance of public policy tends to be conservative and laissez-faire because the private sector is sufficiently robust to create general prosperity.

The economy transitions to where circuit two dominates when business concerns shift from increasing investment to earn profit from new endeavors, to making more profit from already existing industries. Dominance of circuit two is evidenced when the economy's cyclical character becomes clear. Discontent arises as economic conditions and opportunities deteriorate, thus income disparities garner more popular attention. Public policy responds by becoming activist, employing fiscal, monetary, and regulatory means to address economic problems. The 1970s and 1980s were times of a circuit two dominance, as were the 1890s and 1930s.

Given the important connection among profitability, investment, and economic activity, a profitability indicator can be used to assess which circuit is most prevalent at any given time. Rising profitability suggests that the forces propelling circuit one dominate those of circuit two. A circuit two dominance is indicated when profitability reaches a plateau and declines. Circuit one and two combine to produce cyclical profitability, and ultimately cycles in employment and output. Turning points in profitability eventually lead to turning points in economic activity.

One such profitability indicator that incorporates a type of income distribution measure is the division of total business profit by total wages paid to labor. Let this variable be called the PW ratio or indicator. The advantage to this measure is that it captures changes in revenues and costs that together determine profit, and marks the distribution of national income between property and labor. Relative movements in sales revenue and the most important cost element, wages paid to labor, measure expansions and squeezes in investment profitability. A rising PW signifies growing cash flows to finance investment, a favorable outlook for continued investment, and that earnings from investing are rising. Alternatively, a falling ratio implies less internal funds, an unfavorable outlook, and less earnings on investment. And the dual role of wages is taken into account as well. Wages as costs affect the amount of profit that businesses realize. Wages also finance consumer spending and as such are a demand factor affecting sales and profit. Similarly, any change in the distribution of national income that affects profitability would be reflected in the PW ratio. Wages are given a magnified impact on the PW ratio because changes in wages affect both the numerator and denominator of the indicator.

Within these larger swings in activity, the economy moves through short run cycles. In short run recoveries, ample productive capacity exists and prices move up in advance of costs, increasing profitability. During recoveries, the number of investment projects increases and entrepreneurial expectations about risk and profits become favorable. Capital spending picks up, productivity improves, and bank lending accommodates higher corporate and consumer borrowing. Monetary and fiscal policy are expansionary, and deregulation and the opening of new domestic and international markets bolsters optimism and stimulates competition. Net deficit spending and money creation fuel more spending and raise profitability further. While the social and institutional setting can vary substantially from one recovery to the next, private and public policy will attempt to create a positive climate for investment.

Cycle expansions end when conditions contrary to those that exist at the beginning arise. Capacity constraints develop and interest rates and wages move up as credit and labor markets tighten. Simultaneously, total demand is held back. Acceptable investment opportunities decline and surplus inventories mount, putting downward pressure on prices and investment. Increased income inequality, by raising the amount of savings relative to income, contributes to a consumption demand insufficient to sustain business sales. Business optimism fades and some reluctance exits to take risks. Rising input costs and declining revenues squeeze profits. Investment and employment fall, eventually creating a negative multiplier and recession.[8]

The graph below shows how profitability (P) and GDP move over the cycle. The data for both variables are computed as index values over six business cycles dating back to the 1950s. Each index number represents a value relative to the mean for each of the two series, namely profits and GDP, at nine distinct points or stages across the business cycle. Stage 1 represents the beginning of recovery, stage 5 is the peak of the cycle, and stage 9 represents the end of recession. The empirical evidence on profitability demonstrates that profits rise in early and mid economic expansion, peak in stage 4, one stage before the peak in GDP, and profits fall throughout recession which begins in stage six. Evidence demonstrates that GDP always ends the cycle higher than it began, but profits can fall substantially, even below where it began the cycle.

---

[8] Note the central role played by profit and investment in generating long run and short run business cycles.

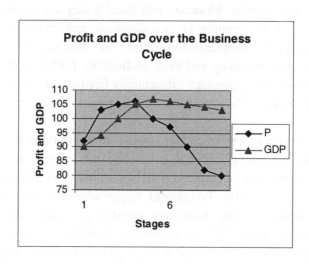

Financial Cycles

Complicating and complementing these swings in business activity are financial cycles. Finance can promote and destabilize the economy. First, finance affects business by determining the cost of external funds. As financing costs fall relative to business cash flows, investment is promoted, but rising costs can curtail investment. Commitment of banks to business matters, as strong commitment is expressed in easy loan terms and willingness to refinance. Finance can affect long-term investment yield projections made by business. Stable and rising stock prices tend to boost investment because they suggest higher expected future returns on capital investment. Stock market volatility and declining share prices undercut investment by creating pessimistic return expectations. Wall Street commitment of funds is exemplified by *relationship investing* where financiers and corporate executives plan investment. But if the financial community is bent on speculation and trading, and has force in corporate governance, it can destabilize investment. When Wall Street's volatile market valuations of firms supercede the more entrepreneurially generated assessments of investment profitability by business, investment may be misdirected and reduced.[9]

Investment must be financed and firms opt for internal funds first because they are the least costly. Typically debt financing is employed next with equity finance the most costly source selected last. Firms in a hedge financing position are in a relatively low risk position because cash flows exceed financing costs. A more risky situation is called speculative finance, where a firm's financing costs exceed, in the short run, its cash flow. The company borrows to meet spending commitments. The worst position is ponzi finance where a firm must increase its borrowing each period to meet spending and debt commitments. Debt financing becomes an ever-larger portion of investment and cash flows are not expected to cover payment commitments over the long run.

Debt and equity financing costs rise as firms move from hedge to ponzi positions. The pace of investment quickens as deficit spending drives profitability, improving the economy's overall fortunes. Rising property values and stock prices increase business access to credit, further promoting investment. Aggregate corporate financial situations determine whether general macroeconomic conditions are robust or fragile. In early and mid expansion, most firms in the economy are in hedge or moderately speculative positions, imparting stability to the economy. But as the typical cycle proceeds, downward pressure on profitability curtails cash flows. Rising interest rates, elevated by private creditors and Federal Reserve policy, add to the carrying cost of bank loans and outstanding bonds. Equity prices continue to rise well into late expansion but eventually turn down, raising external financing costs further. Collateral values decline, depressing investment and lending. The general economy moves progressively from a hedge to a speculative and onto a ponzi financial position. This changing financial fortune in the business sector afflicts the financial sector, as more banks and finance companies possess greater leverage and depressed stock prices.

---

[9] See the seminal works of Minsky [1986] and Keynes [1964] on the importance of finance in modern capitalism.

A financial crisis can now strike, reflected in an intense demand for credit and desire to liquidate positions. Falling business profitability undermines companies' ability to pay dividends and interest expenses, and banks and other financial institutions raise loan standards and costs, often prompted by business bankruptcies that increase portfolio risk. Just the expectation of heightened risk can lead to higher rates. The Federal Reserve may hike rates to stem inflation. These actions push more firms into speculative or ponzi positions. Financial distress encourages firms to cut investment to free up cash flow for debt payments. Recession results.[10]

Explaining the 1990s Expansion

It's now time to summarize our theory. The economy moves through long and short run business cycles. Profitability and investment are interdependent, and these two principal variables create a cyclical economy. Financing costs affect the ability of firms to fund investment and generate profits. Profits, wages, and interest generated from economic activity affect future investment and society's income distribution. One measure of income distribution is the PW ratio. An economic environment forms a context for investment, profits, and finance; in general the environment will either promote or dissuade growth by affecting profit incentives, spending, and expectations of business and banking. The stage of the business cycle influences the economic environment. Net deficit spending and money creation are necessary for growth.

The decade of the 1990s was one where the economic environment and financial structure were conducive to growth. Early in the decade, monetary policy drove down interest rates, and corporate raiding subsided, allowing for a shift back to less speculation and more long run investment. Corporate policy promoted restructuring and adoption of new technology to improve

---

[10] See Wolfson's text *Financial Crises* for a review of post war financial crises and their causes. Another excellent analysis of banking crises is found in Randall [1993]. See also Hyman Minsky, *Stabilizing An Unstable Economy*, Yale University Press, 1986.

profitability and efficiency. Government budget deficits remained high to foster spending. Throughout the decade, a positive business climate prevailed, optimism led to the creation of new businesses and investment, and Wall Street promoted mergers and stockholdings among a wider portion of the public. Money manager capitalism came into full force.[11] By the decade's end, consumer optimism, growing incomes and low unemployment, and unprecedented stock price enhancement fostered growing consumer sector budget deficits.[12]

And quite interestingly, greater income inequality has promoted economy-wide net deficits. The expansions of the last two decades resulted in an income dispersion that greatly magnified the incomes of the top twenty percent relative to the bottom sixty percent of the population. A simultaneous stock market boom elevated the net worth of millions. Together, these developments facilitated much greater credit-driven consumption and investment, predicated on increased borrowing capacities and increased credit needs. Larger net worth produced a wealth effect that in turn produced sustained net private-sector deficits. And ironically the very same income inequality, expressed in generation-long declines in real incomes for many Americans, induced the upper half of middle income Americans in particular to raise their borrowing [Maki and Palumbo 2001] to maintain or raise living standards. Enhanced consumer borrowing created outlets for the savings of the affluent and strong profit and employment growth resulted.[13]

The lesson of the 1990s boom is clear: Any prolonged expansion of business and banking profits concurrent with restrictive government budget policy necessitates unavoidable and unsustainable prolonged increases in

---

[11] This particular institution will be fully described in later chapters.

[12] The seminal work on measuring cash flows and analysis of 1990s growth is by Godley [1999].

[13] Moreover, as credit extension reached down to the lower income classes, very effective business marketing practices encouraged greater demand for funds. The financial sector is quite efficient at finding outlets for the savings bestowed upon them and businesses are quite adept at promoting mass consumption in this era by providing people with products that create new "personal identities" or services that create life altering "experiences." And due to the expansion of the service economy, a labor-intensive sector, unemployment falls to a thirty year low.

private sector debt. And the more unequal the income distribution, the more that firms and consumers must borrow to sustain growth. The graphic below demonstrates that private sector spending growth has generally outpaced income growth in the 1990s, especially in the late 1990s, and it was this spending-income gap that accelerated economic growth at the end of the decade.

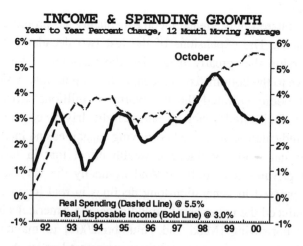

INCOME & SPENDING GROWTH
Year to Year Percent Change, 12 Month Moving Average

Real Spending (Dashed Line) @ 5.5%
Real, Disposable Income (Bold Line) @ 3.0%

Source: First Union Bank

What could end the expansion of the 1990s? Three possible scenarios avail themselves. (1) The demise of the wealth effect would disrupt the continuous spending and borrowing increases of much of the public, leading to a curtailment in business investment and profit; (2) Rising interest and other expenses would stop further advance in private sector deficits, as income would be diverted to pay debt servicing and other costs; and (3) Declining corporate investment and profitability would negatively affect both employment and financial markets. A drop in investment would create a poorer profit picture, leading to spending cuts by households and business as unemployment rises. Lower profits would also create falling stock prices that end the wealth effect. Without public policy intervention, a negative multiplier would generate further declines in economic activity.[14]

By Spring 2001, scenario three appears to be developing. A cyclical downturn in profitability appears to be occurring, as evidenced by the graph below.

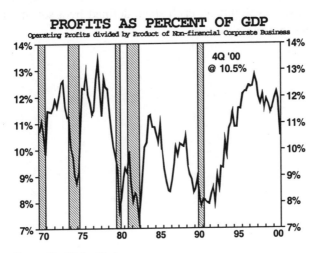

PROFITS AS PERCENT OF GDP
Operating Profits divided by Product of Non-financial Corporate Business

Source: First Union Bank

Conclusion

Business investment drives profit and innovation, and in turn profits reward investment. Profits and investment move within short run and longer run cycles, and these cycles are largely driven by the internal workings of the

---

[14] The economic boom of the 1990s has had a conservative influence on public policy and public thinking. Unprecedented private sector deficits produced sufficient economic stimuli to offset the negative consequences emanating from high interest rates, government retrenchment, free trade, and industry and income concentration. Politicians and the public now believe that elitist policies work to expand output, employment, and opportunities, and that more of these policies are essential.

economy. The backdrop for business, characterized in part by the socio-political environment and the state of psychology and confidence, can assist or hinder development. The division of profits and wages in national income, one measure of income distribution, is a cycle indicator and is influenced by the economic environment. But capitalism does not remain the same system over time; it evolves institutionally and hence in behavior. Capitalism moves through stages of development, each stage defined by a set of attributes. It is to this issue that we now turn.

Chapter 4

Stages of Capitalism

The U.S. economy has transited through four distinct stages. The agrarian-handicraft era and merchant capitalism dominated colonial and early America, and gave way to industrial capitalism, beginning with the introduction of the railroad. Finance capitalism followed presiding over two great merger waves and the 1920s boom. Managerial capitalism replaced finance capitalism, as the latter fundamentally contributed to the stock market crash and great depression. Executive domination of the firm, supported by state policy, lasted through the 1970s. Since that time, a new and as of yet not fully understood stage has come upon the scene. Large pension and mutual funds, typically run by major security firms and banks, are affecting corporate governance and macroeconomic conditions. There appears to be some change in the way finance affects investment and the business cycle, and the issue of income inequality is once again front and center.

Agrarian-Handicraft System

The first important economic era for the United States is the agrarian-handicraft system, dating from the colonial period to the 1830s and represents a pre-capitalist stage for the United States. In this era, the American economy is overwhelmingly agricultural, consisting of many small family farms, with artisans and a small professional class working closely with the farm sector or in towns. Small farms and firms produce either for self-sufficiency or for local markets. Enterprises rely principally on internal funds to finance investment, and bank loans to finance inventories and goods in transit. The quantity of money was limited, often in the form of precious metals or foreign coins, and typically people bartered and relied on reciprocal obligations to conduct business, not contracts. Enterprise was a "way of life", and within the firm, control and ownership were integrated, and therefore saving and investment were done by the same people. Most enterprises were family run and very small.

The first stage of capitalism, Merchant capitalism, existed along side the agrarian-handicraft system. In urban colonial America and the United States, a more commercial, market oriented economy operated. In this portion of the economy, merchant and commercial banks financed primarily proprietorships and partnerships in acquiring inventories or in the production of goods. Economic activity centered on the buying and selling of goods. Production is carried out in the home and in small firms. The putting-out system is employed. An acquisitive ethic to accumulate wealth and capital, and a desire for economic expansion, contrasts markedly with the more traditional, cooperative agrarian society. A reliance on local sources and personal relationships for investment funds resulted in an emphasis on local projects; there was nothing resembling a national market for capital. Government operations were very limited, but in the early years of the Republic, government financed the construction of turnpikes and canals. The economy's money supply was in the form of precious metals and state bank notes.[1]

The slave economy of the American South contrasted sharply with the merchant-market economy of the North and seacoast. Technology, climate, racism, and the lure of profits in cotton and other staples pushed the South to a long run commitment to agriculture and slavery. While not wholly rejecting industrialization, an economy built on an agrarian-slave base retarded modernization and economic development. It also limited integration of the North with the South. Irreconcilable disputes over the preservation and extension of slavery, and the decline of Southern influence in national politics, led to a civil war that unified the nation and redirected Southern economic evolution along capitalist lines.

---

[1] The work by Szatmary [1980] contrasts the rural traditional economy with the urban commercial economy of New England in the 1780s.

Industrial Capitalism

Stage two or industrial capitalism began around the time of the advent of railroads and the telegraph in the 1840s and lasted until about 1900. A new ethic or spirit sanctioned accumulation, and risk taking was balanced with discipline and hopefulness. This era was the age of the entrepreneur, corporate robber barons, and industrial development. Increasingly, businesses expanded in size and produced for regional and national markets. Merchant capital was invested increasingly into manufacturing. Competitive price pressures and new technologies led firms to exploit economies of scale. Moreover, transportation improvements and growing national capital markets fostered the arrival of big business. The corporate form of business became the preferred accumulation devise, amassing ever-larger amounts of people and capital. The factory and mass production were the mainstays of this period. While doing business remained "a way of life", wealth accumulation became an end in itself. Banks remained short-term providers of credit but retained-earnings from operations were the main source of funds for expansion. Government supplemented private money to finance railroad construction and frontier settlement.[2] Vested interests in the firm were motivated towards the long run success of the business. This period is one of high investment and growth, but the economy is increasingly subject to business cycles and financial panics. Stage two was marked by laissez-faire public policy. The arrival of large enterprise facilitated accumulation and produced a much more unequal society.

Finance Capitalism

Stage three or finance capitalism runs from the late 1890s to the mid 1930s. This era is noted for the nationalization of capital markets. Leading financial institutions promoted the allocation of capital based on competitive rates of

---

[2] Myers [1970] provides detail of the importance of public and private finance before the Civil War.

return as opposed to the funding of local endeavors via personal relationships. Industrial fortunes provide significant savings pools to tap into. Improvements in financial intermediation contribute to increased levels of saving and investment. Life insurance companies and most importantly investment banks provide increased long term funding. Finance capitalism is noted for the powerful influence of investment bankers in corporate affairs and the consolidation of the country's most economically important firms into more stable, less competitive, oligopolistic industries. Investment bankers and industrialists govern the nation's first mega-enterprises.[3]

Three important institutional changes affecting investment arise in this period. First, conflict arose between the economic interests of the financial and industrial sectors over the distribution of profit. Industrial capitalists are rewarded with profit for investing and risk-taking, but financiers had a claim to the firm's earnings given their role in providing external finance and fostering corporate consolidations.

Second, within major businesses, ownership separated from control. Increasingly large, diverse, and complex enterprises required professional management teams to administer operations. Stockholders became larger in number and less influential in company affairs as their knowledge about operations was inadequate and their holdings represented a small fraction of the outstanding equities. Separation brought about a divergence of interest between owners and management, and resulted in the splitting of two important functions into two separate processes. The financing-speculation process and the investment-enterprise process were undertaken by different groups, namely financiers of the former and management of the latter.

The third important change was the rise of an organized stock exchange. Participants in this sector were interested in trading and speculation with a focus on short-term gains. In combination with volatile sentiments, their commitments to firms were revocable. Fickle assessments of corporate profitability, as expressed in the Stock Exchange's valuation of firms, substituted for long run, more rational assessments produced by business

---

[3] The identification of important institutional attributes of capitalism's first three stages comes from Puth [1982].

insiders. Stage-three capitalism was marked by intensified periods of financial instability, severe economic downturns, and income inequality.[4]

Managerial Capitalism

Managerial capitalism, stage four in the evolution of the economy, runs from the mid 1930s through the 1970s. Stock market speculation and financial pyramiding of companies, the Great Depression, and the subsequent economic reforms of the 1930s, facilitated the managerial revolution. These changes diminished the importance of finance in affecting macroeconomic conditions and corporate governance. Along with the securities and banking regulation of the New Deal, managerial dominance and independence arose because of the separation of ownership from control. Increasingly, stockholders became a diversified, numerous, and unorganized body of people, insufficiently informed, to effect change within the firm. Stockholder interest was in earning income, and lowering portfolio risk through liquidity and diversification, not governance.[5] And importantly, a sufficient level of internal funds for investment and low borrowing costs provide for managerial financial autonomy. Growth and stability are prominent goals of corporate executives. Corporate planning and politicking are employed to significantly influence markets.

An active, interventionist State promoted business sales and profits by maintaining low interest rates, by deficit spending, and by forging the expansion of international markets. Functional finance budgeting provided the fiscal means to maintain a jobs target of high employment. Large Cold

---

[4] The major institutional characteristics of the economy during the nineteenth and early twentieth centuries have been thoroughly described by such important contributors as Berle and Means [1932], Means [1933], Weber [1994], Keynes [1964], and Minsky [1990]. Recent reviews of Keynes' theory of development stages include the works of James Crotty [1990B] and Karl McDermott [1993]. For a recent review of Minsky's work see Whalen [1997].

[5] Along with the study by Berle and Means, the prominent works covering the managerial firm and corporate governance are Galbraith (1967), Baran and Sweezy [1966], Chandler [1977], Herman [1981], Nicholas Wolfson [1984], and Minsky [1990].

War–social welfare spending budgets were complemented by an expanding administrative management function that directs resources, and supervises and regulates private sector activity.[6] Economic growth, unions, and government policy work together to build a large middle class and reduce poverty.

Another important element of this stage was the internationalization of industrial and finance capital. The expansionist drive of managerially controlled firms led industry and banking to establish production facilities and financial institutions abroad. The internationalization of capital flows, commercial banking, and investment banking expedited direct foreign investment. The penetration of multinational business and finance created national economic interdependence and forced evolution on existing institutions in non-capitalist, less developed nations.[7] The growth in size and market extension of nonfinancial corporations pushed banks to accommodate need for larger loan size. Branch banking and bank holding companies develop to meet these financing demands. Banks themselves increase their funding by selling more stock.

Federal Reserve policy facilitated government finance and private sector borrowing during this period. The Depression had established low interest rates when credit demand collapsed. The Central Bank maintained low interest rates during World War Two to assist government's prosecution of the war. Following the war, the Fed continued to support bond prices, producing low and stable interest rates, by purchasing government debt.

U.S. capitalism underwent a transition beginning in the 1970s. Deterioration in the economic interests of the financial sector was one factor that initiated the transition. Two major spikes in oil prices and a wage-price spiral pushed up inflation rates that depreciated the value of currency and debt. Interest rates became less than inflation rates. These events prompted efforts by the financial community to enhance their economic and political

---

[6] See the work of Walker and Vatter [1997] for a comprehensive history on the rise of big government.

[7] See the works of Heilbroner [1985] and DuBoff [1989] on the internationalization of capital.

power as evidenced in a more aggressive, independent, and restrictive Federal Reserve monetary policy.[8] New technologies and global interdependence and competition affected corporate economics as well. These developments conspired to put downward pressure on corporate profit rates, market shares, and stock prices. In addition to restrictive monetary policy to keep interest rates higher, major bond and stockholders sought to elevate their influence in corporate governance to enhance their monetary returns. By the 1980s, financiers played increasingly important roles as funders of corporate takeovers and advocates of restructurings to boost equity values and dividend payouts. Corporate raiders often raised debt-to-equity levels in firms to discipline their spending habits and to prompt increased payments to shareholders.[9]

Recent Institutional Developments

Major developments in modern times have worked interdependently to transform the American economy once again. Important structural changes are identified and analyzed by such noted and varied scholars as Reich (1992), Drucker (1993, 1995), Thurow (1992, 1996), D'Arista (2000), and Wolman and Colamosca (1997). These changes have contributed to much dynamism and opportunity, but have also reversed the gains made in the prior stage in moderating inequality. The important developments are listed below:

(1) *Globalization*: National economies are integrating and becoming increasingly interdependent. Resources more easily and quickly flow across borders. Ending of capital controls and increased cross-border transactions fostered the rise of portfolio investment. Firms are increasingly transnational, producing where production costs are relatively low and selling where prices

---

[8] See the views of Dugger [1993] and Galbraith [1996] on the resurgence of financial sector power.

[9] Blair's [1995] text provides a comprehensive look at corporate control and governance.

are the highest. Governments compete for corporate investment, and direct significant effort to forming economic unions and free trade zones. Corporate profits are higher in part from use of low wage labor in third world nations and from the opening of centrally planned economies to capitalist penetration. Competition among the world's professional and educated workers for employment will put downward pressure on their incomes.

(2) *Increased Competition*: Competitive pressures are intensified as companies from many different countries vie for consumers and workers. Competition has encouraged capital investment and organizational innovation. American companies have reestablished their world class competitive status by restructuring and reengineering. While competition has resulted in many economic winners, pressure toward the equalization of world wages has concentrated income and depressed or stagnated living standards for many. Disinflation is the norm with some deflation in producer and commodity prices. Companies are shifting from cost-plus pricing to price-led costing.

(3) *Employment Sector Shift*: An increasing amount of output and particularly jobs derive from the service and information technology sectors. Greater demands exist for a skill- and knowledge- based labor force, which must constantly train and retrain. Bureaucratic streamlining, horizontal management, and work-teams characterize some of the more creative firms. Self-employment and entrepreneurial upstarts are more common. Difference in opportunities and income, and premiums paid for education, are separating Americans along economic class and education lines. Business curriculums penetrate the fields of health care, engineering, and education. Unions have declined in importance and more work is done on a temporary or contract basis.

(4) *Role of Government*: Public policy is now more fiscally conservative and pro-business. State spending and activism are eschewed and efforts to cut business regulations are stressed. A slow deterioration in social safety nets is underway. Government must reinvent itself and make efforts to improve education and infrastructure. The independence of Federal Reserve policy is affirmed, resulting in relatively high real interest rates and an emphasis on controlling inflation. Fiscal policy should promote balanced or surplus budgets

to increase savings to the private sector. State-owned enterprises are to be sold to private interests and some state functions contracted out to private business.

(5) *A Multi-polar World*: Much of the former socialist world is integrating with a global capitalist economy. Major institutional and legal overhauls are necessary in many countries, requiring adjustment and learning by millions of people. Some third-world nations are approaching first and second world status. While one military superpower exists, no one country or region will dictate world trading rules. Central banks and international institutions such as the IMF are active stabilizers of world financial markets. The "Washington Consensus" model of free trade and currency flows, and deregulation, is increasingly adopted by Emerging Market economies.

Conclusion

The developments noted above are transforming economic and political life. But another significant institutional change is affecting corporate governance and finance, and in combination with the above noted changes, is fashioning a fifth stage in American capitalist evolution. Major non-bank financial institutions, such as pension and mutual funds, are now important financiers and owners of corporate America. This is the era of money manager capitalism. This newest era of capitalist development, like the eras before it, has specific attributes and implications for economic performance and public policy. It defines the current economic environment. These matters are addressed in the next section.

Chapter 5

Money Manager Capitalism

American capitalism has entered a fifth stage of development. Evolution from managerial capitalism to money manager capitalism is spurred by the rise of large institutional holders of savings capital such as pension and mutual funds. Very gradually, these financial institutions have accumulated large holdings of securities from the largest and most important corporations in the United States. This chapter is based upon such authorities as Hyman Minsky, William Dugger, and Charles Whalen who originated the idea of money manager capitalism, and makes the case that the U.S. economy has undergone significant change in the 1980s and 1990s. This section of the book reaffirms and strengthens the argument that money manager capitalism is a reality and that this institution of capitalism is actually just one dimension of a larger evolutionary process of change for the American economy. Money manager capitalism is affecting the flow of funds in ways that can stabilize and promote business investment and at other times, slow investment and stagnate the economy.

Institutional Evolution

As noted by economists such as Lester Thurow and Robert Reich, and management expert Peter Drucker, major institutional changes have occurred in the U.S. economy in the last twenty years. These authors discuss the onset and effects of globalization, increased domestic and international competition, the growing service, high technology, knowledge and skill based economy, and of the decline in public sector responsibilities and activism.

These scholars delineate a new era in capitalism. Within the context of these structural changes, one additional significant institutional development is money manager capitalism. The following facts and observations evidence this evolutionary development:

Financial institutions, especially pension and mutual funds, hold separately and in conjunction with one another large blocks of individual company stocks and bonds, making these institutions the principal owners of major corporations and financiers of business investment. These institutions have acquired effective voting rights, influence over directors, and the ability to significantly alter a firm's financing costs and market value.[1] These institutional asset holders challenge executive compensation plans, corporate board make-ups, and corporate bylaws that protect management from takeovers. Large volumes of capital are placed in accordance with longer run strategies by funds whose clients are saving for retirement or to meet other long-term objectives. More savers and money managers now believe that in the long run, the return on stocks is higher and the riskiness of stocks is lower than bonds. This drives the demand for equities.[2] Financial institutions are also more aware of their potential power and more aware of their responsibility to large numbers of clients. In-house research and close contact with companies they back make these institutions more informed and willing to act to affect corporate governance. Major corporations make considerable efforts to attract institutional support and maintain investor relations departments.

And financial and nonfinancial firms are increasingly intertwined. Their portfolios consist of a mixture of capital and financial assets. Nonfinancial firms are more dependent on interest income and deal extensively in currency trading and financial derivatives. Financial firms are responsible for a larger percentage of investment. Financial and nonfinancial firms are now major financiers of venture capital companies that purchase equities in start-up

---

[1] On these matters, see the Wall Street Journal (WSJ) June 28, 1990 page CI and WSJ September 22, 1992 page A42. Brown (1998) and Useem [1996] explore the extent of institutional holdings.

[2] See the work of Glassman and Hassett [1999].

firms that foster competition and innovation. These venture capital companies take active positions in management and tie management interests to stockholder interests.[3] This closer association between finance and commerce is evidenced by increased stock buybacks, dividend payments, and mergers that push funds into Wall Street and financial institutions, who in turn allocate the funds back into stock and bond markets or into new stock offerings. Some firms issue debt capital to fund stock repurchases. This symbiosis enhances fund flows between the sectors and limits the supply of stock to maintain asset values. And the larger fraction of Americans participating in retirement plans creates a broader base of interest in and consistent support for stock buying and building portfolios.

Moreover, regulatory changes have expanded the rights of major stockholders to influence company decisions. This influence occurs through expanded rights to shareholder lists and to place resolutions on ballots, and through financier groups that discuss company matters. Management's domination of the proxy machinery has been weakened by new SEC rules.[4] And lastly, bank legislation passed in the 1990s permits interstate banking and financial asset conglomeration. This legislation will foster the development of multifaceted mega-financial institutions, furthering the concentration of savings, and giving these firms added influence in corporate governance.

Implications of Money Manager Capitalism

Some economists such as Whalen [1997] have made the case that money manager capitalism has created negative social and economic implications by narrowing the focus of corporate governance to enhancement of shareholder value. Major financial institutions are pushing firms into mergers

---

[3] See the work of Parker and Parker (1998) and the National Public Radio (NPR) Report [1999].

[4] The text by Blair [1995] covers regulatory changes on pages 70-74 and provides and in-depth discussion of corporate governance issues.

and acquisitions, restructurings, and disinvestment in domestic operations, to raise earnings per share at the expense of workers and communities. Concern exists that corporations are now focused on shorter-term financial performance criteria and not long-term investment, resulting in damage to U.S. firms' ability to globally compete and meet social needs. These are important microeconomic issues.

This chapter addresses the macroeconomic ramifications of money manager capitalism. In particular, what affect will money manager capitalism have on economic stability? It's likely that the current era of money manager capitalism is producing a more stable macroeconomic system. In general, three important attributes of our new economic era tend to promote stability: First, disinflation and deflation characterize the U.S. economy and the international system in the 1990s and beyond. Second, major financial institutions have diversified holdings of corporate financial assets, and a merger wave in the financial sector is occurring. And third, money manager capitalism promotes a new relationship between corporate investors and their financiers. Let's look at these in some detail.

Lester Thurow argues that inflation is an "extinct volcano".[5] The war against inflation of the 1970s and 1980s was won not by tight monetary policy but when the factors that created inflation went away. Oil prices collapsed with the weakening of OPEC and the rise of many oil producing countries. Managed care and Medicare spending cuts have caused health care inflation to abate. World unemployment and capacity matter more than U.S. measures, and world statistics indicate excess capacity. Many firms outsource and invest in new technology to cut costs and prices. Downward pressures exist on U.S. and world real wages. Electronic commerce has increased competition, and by reducing inventory and real estate costs, E-commerce allows firms to reduce prices. This suggests that in the 1990s and beyond, there will be less frequent need for the Federal Reserve to raise interest rates to curb inflation. Central Banks will by matter of practical

---

[5] See Thurow's text "The Future of Capitalism" [1996] chapter 9. Also read Business Week 1999, page 30.

importance be more concerned with developing country financial crises and slow growth in developed countries than with inflation.

Pension and mutual funds routinely own dozens to hundreds of companies' bonds and stocks to diversify portfolios. Hedging strategies are commonly used to offset swings in financial asset values. An increasing portion of money is held in broadly-based index funds. Banks are moving into the securities business through mergers and have won a further relaxation of banking laws to allow for all-service financial conglomerates. Nationwide banking allows for diversified loan portfolios and industry concentration.[6] These developments suggest that the domestic financial sector should experience fewer financial difficulties due to diversified financial portfolios and market power. This implies less frequent need for Federal Reserve lender of last resort operations to stop financial crises.

But most importantly, the financial sector should be a major contributor to stability because of the important economic relations established in money manager capitalism. What has evolved is that larger and larger amounts of money are allocated by large financial conglomerates that have increasingly closer ties to top management who plan business investment. Uniformity in attitude and recognition of common financial interests by firms and their financiers have produced financial institutions who are committed long-run backers of large businesses which account for much of the economy's investment.[7] And this institutional commitment is strengthened as the clients of pension and mutual funds increasingly provide their money with long-term capital appreciation objectives. Moreover, since financial institutions now have more power in corporate governance and more committed money from clients, the ownership and control functions of enterprise are becoming more integrated. Commitment of funds and functional integration should

---

[6] Edwards [1996] and Mayer [1997] document banking trends.

[7] John M. Keynes argued in his text "The General Theory" that Capitalism must restore financier commitment to enterprise. Stock market speculation in the 1920s, he thought, destabilized business investment and led to the Great Depression. Private sector evolution has redesigned the relationship between finance and commerce, and is perhaps providing a means by which to accomplish Keynes' hopes.

bolster entrepreneurial risk taking and optimism by preventing sharp fluctuations in perceived business investment returns.[8] In other words, the above noted developments should stabilize the flow of funds to, and the stock prices of, the business sector, which in turn will promote and stabilize investment, even in the face of falling business profitability or higher interest rates. Furthermore, sustained upward movements in stock prices and PE ratios generate wealth effects that bolster business investment and consumer spending.[9]

If money manager capitalism is an effective force promoting investment, capital spending should be a significant contributor to growth in the 1990s. Evidence shows that along with an increase in corporate profitability and stock prices in the 1990s, and increased money flows to mutual funds, the investment to GDP ratio has risen to a 1999 value of 16.1 percent, higher than what was achieved at the end of the 1980s' expansion and comparable to what was achieved at the end of the expansion in the 1970s. In the 1990s, investment was responsible for 32 percent of the rise in real GDP, and in 1997 and 1998, investment was responsible for 38 percent and 45 percent respectively of the increase in real GDP. Business capital spending in the 1990s has risen above its normal cyclical rise. Capital spending on structures and equipment accounts for 25% of the rise in GDP in the 1990s compared to an 8% contribution in the 1980s, and the percentage change in real investment has consistently exceeded the percent gains in real GDP and real consumption in the 1990s. The only expansion period since World War Two that lasted more than five years without a substantial contribution from

---

[8] As Minsky and Keynes have taught, financial activity can destabilize investment by raising the cost of external financing relative to business cash flows, and by interfering with long term yield projections. The latter is the effect of financial market valuations of firms superceding the internally generated assessments of business investment profitability. See the definitive works of Minsky [1986] and Keynes [1964].

[9] There is no reason to believe that money manager capitalism is so powerful that investment will become acyclical or that the economy will not experience downturns. But money manager capitalism could act as a quasi-floor under, and stabilizer of, investment and stock prices, and investment may be a larger overall contributor to growth.

government spending is the 1990s expansion. This nine year expansion has occurred despite lower real federal spending and high real interest rates, federal budget surpluses, financial crises in developing countries, and a widening trade deficit.[10]

It is clear that technology is a major factor driving investment. Reported business investment would be higher if the national income statistics treated R&D spending that produces intangible assets, like patents, as investment. If so, depreciation would be higher and profits larger, making PE ratios closer to historic averages [Nakamura 1999; Coy 1999]. In late October 1999, the Commerce Department decided to record computer spending as investment.

Furthermore, substantial stock market advances are boosting consumer spending and borrowing by increasing people's net worth. This is called the wealth effect.[11] As demonstrated by Godley and Martin [1999], and Godley and Wray [1999], the financial balance or cash flow position of businesses and households fell sharply throughout the 1990s and turned negative in 1995, while private net borrowing rose substantially. Households are spending

---

[10] Data presented in the Survey of Current Business and the 1998 and 1999 Economic Report of the President demonstrate an increase in the role of investment driving economic growth. Business Week magazine highlights the impact of investment on the current economic expansion. See BW Feb. 15, 1999, pages 30-32, Feb. 22, 1999, pages 30-32, and March 15, 1999, page 22.

[11] Since 1982, the market has risen at a 17% annual rate, compared to a long run historical average of 10%. As of the late 1990s, the breadth of the stock market advance has narrowed and the PEs have risen further. These recent events suggest that the current high stock market valuations are unsustainable. There is also a question as to how reliable the market averages are as gauges of the general stock price performance across the economy when a few large capitalization stocks can move an entire market. Moreover, beginning in November 1999, the Dow Jones Co. withdrew four old-line companies from the Dow index and inserted four prominent economy-leading firms, namely Intel, Microsoft, SBC Communications, and Home Depot. The Dow index has been given a greater upward bias with these additions. Stock prices can fall significantly or become depressed. Many factors affect stock markets. A large downturn in corporate spending and hence profitability could push stock prices much lower and reverse the wealth effect.

more than they are earning by borrowing, stimulating growth, despite tight fiscal and trade stances in the 1990s. Increased wealth is prompting a spending binge. Consumer borrowing is further supported by sub-prime lending, a policy of banks that reduces the collateral and net worth requirements needed by borrowers to obtain loans. This policy enhances the debt-financed spending of the private sector. People and firms now consider higher amounts of debt acceptable and sustainable.

The stock market performance of the 1980s and 1990s demonstrates a commitment of savings capital to consistent purchases of stock. Market gains are frequently 50 to 100 point daily advances, and higher than normal yearly percentage gains of above twenty percent, are common during the current era. Such advances occur without any increase in volatility. The number of days per year that the Dow's closing price changed by more than two percent either way was about the same in the 1990s as in the 1970s and 1980s.[12]

Students of modern corporate governance have all noted the increased attention by executives of nonfinancial corporations to shareholder value and the greater influence of financial institutions in corporate governance.[13] Accepting this suggests that corporate financial policy of the 1980s and 1990s should favor stockholders and that mutual and pension funds have greater commitment to and interest in corporate equities. Empirically we should expect higher dividend pay-outs and price-earnings ratios to accompany money manager capitalism. Dividend pay-outs are up since the 1970s. Dividends paid out of after tax corporate income averaged 36.5% in the 1970s, but 61.1% and 65.9% in the 1980s and 1990s respectively. Kopcke's [1992] study shows a revival in PEs in the late 1980s, and in the 1990s, PEs on major averages were running from the mid to high 20s which are in excess of historic norms which range from about 12 to 18. Trailing PEs for

---

[12] Volatility figures are supplied by the Public TV program "Wall Street Week" on August 6, 1999.

[13] For example, see Blair's text *Ownership and Control* published in 1995 by the Brookings Institution.

the S&P 500 index are typically above 20 in the 1990s. Additionally, net interest payments as a portion of national income are up from the two to three percent range, three to four decades ago, to the six to ten percent range in the 1980s and 1990s.

There are however dimensions to money manager capitalism that could be problematic. For many years there has been an ongoing decline in the importance of the banking industry as a financial intermediary relative to mutual and pension funds and financial conglomerates.[14] The significance of the growing importance of nonbank intermediation of funds to finance investment is that these institutions do not create money, as traditional bank lending does, but simply allocate what has been saved. Yet investment that is financed entirely by current savings cannot produce growth. Only aggregate net deficit spending produces growth by augmenting incomes and balance sheets, and this requires money creation. Money growth depends on private sector credit demand, which in turn depends on business profitability and aggregate demand. Yet, the source of business debt financing will increasingly be savings capital raised from the financial markets, not new money created from loans which are in turn based on the banking systems' creation of deposits. The relative decline of bank money creation suggests that money growth rates will be somewhat low and the money that does exist will move faster through the economy during expansions. In turn, as interest rates are kept high, macroeconomic performance could exhibit low growth rates generally and at times stagnation or recession due to the restraint on the demand for borrowed money.

And the evidence suggests that traditional commercial banking is in a relative decline. Nonfinancial borrowing from banks and thrifts has fallen since the mid 1970s to a modern-day low of 22% and 9% respectively. Commercial bank share of total financial assets has fallen from 41% to 29% over the 1970 to 1994 period [Edwards 1996, 12–13, 15]. Mutual fund assets are now greater than total bank assets [Federal Reserve Bulletin 1998]. The financial sector is economizing on liquid money balances. Both MI

---

[14] This development is documented by Fortune [1997] and Edwards [1996].

transaction – and MI income – velocity have risen since the 1960s. MI income velocity stopped its secular increase in the early 1980s and turned cyclical until resuming its upward trend in the mid 1990s. It's now at a modern high of 7.8 in mid 1998. M1 money growth rates are lower in the 1990s' expansion than in the 1980s' expansion. Growth rates decline from 7.4% to 3.8% respectively.[15] A tight monetary policy and attention to price stability have put upward pressure on real interest rates. Real short and long-term interest rates are notably higher since the late 1970s. And despite very low consumer price inflation and producer goods price deflation in the late 1990s, intermediate and long rates on government and corporate bonds remain relatively high compared to the pre-1979 period [Wolman and Colamosca 1997].

Another tendency toward stagnation could arise from the growing income and wealth inequality to which money manager capitalism has contributed. Many studies in the 1980s and 1990s demonstrate that income dispersion has increased and in general, roughly the top twenty percent of the population has received the significant majority of higher real incomes and wealth. Money manager capitalism assisted wealth concentration by encouraging corporate restructurings and global investment, and by distributing money management services and savings vehicles principally to those individuals who have seen the biggest income gains. Much of the economy's output growth and asset price increases in the last two decades were driven by the spending and risk-taking of higher income earners. Thus what has developed is an economy overly dependent on a relatively small group whose spending inclinations may be dampened by lower profits and/or stock prices. Spending reductions would lead to a general fall in aggregate demand and an economic downturn. People will prefer to hold their wealth in cash and not spend, making a revival in economic activity, spurred by the private sector, unlikely.

Moreover, there is interdependence between most Americans on the one hand and affluent Americans on the other. Growing inequality in this stage of capitalism has prompted the bottom two-thirds of Americans to spend

---

[15] The Federal Reserve Bulletin and the Survey of Current Business report such data.

more, by borrowing more and saving less in order to maintain living standards, thereby driving the profits and stock prices of the affluent. Wealthier Americans are spending but also saving much and reaping the rewards of asset price appreciation, yet the continued spending of most Americans depends on continued good profit and stock price performance of the affluent. Any disruption in the spending of much of the public or any curtailment in business investment and job creation by the affluent would negatively affect aggregate economic performance. The economy will remain vulnerable to this interdependency between the income classes and between the financial and business sectors.

Stage Comparison

The table below provides a summary of key attributes of the most recent stage, managerial capitalism, with money manager capitalism.

Monetary Policy during the Fifth Stage

Money Manager Capitalism is about a renewed commitment of finance towards investment and business. A strong, long term demand for stocks coupled with limits on the supply of stock, keep stock prices high and advancing. Economic weakness, brought on by a decline in business profitability, is likely to create stock market volatility and/or price declines. But the current stage of capitalism is one where finance is more supportive of commerce than what prevailed in the early twentieth century. Large financial institutions and individuals desire long term capital appreciation, and maintenance of high values, not just on stocks but bonds as well. Though bond yields may be relatively high on new companies, profitable performance and a track record should bring rates down and prices up on these assets. Given this, the current monetary policy regime is not consistent with money manager capitalism. A Classically driven policy places upward pressure on rates to contain inflation and slow economic growth, creating potential for a financial crisis, which of course is destructive to bond price appreciation.

	Managerial Capitalism	Money Manager Capitalism
The major activity financed	Growth and Stability	The New Economy and Globalization
The major source of finance	Commercial Banks and the Central Bank	Pension and Mutual Funds
Ownership/Control Link	Separation of Ownership from Control; stock trading and short term thinking	Integration of Ownership and Control; long term commitment of funds
The dominant economic Enterprise financed	Corporate Conglomerates	Transnational Corporations
Locus of power	Corporate Board and Executives	Money Fund Managers and Corporate Executives
The dominant economic input	Corporate planning and government regulation	Corporate planning combined with expertise in finance
Monetary policy regime in practice	Low interest rate, counter cyclical policy	High interest rate, counter cyclical policy
Government policy in force	Deficit spending, counter cyclical policy	Balanced budget, pro business spending, free trade policy
Financial Structure	Generally robust	Generally robust but subject to fragility
Economic Goals	Contained competition, long run investment view, growth, and job security	Increased competition, long run investment view, growth, innovation, and job insecurity

Note: The above table was inspired by Charles Whalen's presentation on money manager capitalism at the Levy Institute's Hyman Minsky Conference, April 1999.

Rate hikes are quickly administered at the first sight of an economically robust business sector or inflation, and this puts downward pressure on bond prices. Bond prices are allowed to rise only when business slumps and rates must be moved down to revive business activity.

We therefore have an ongoing conflict between current institutional evolution and a monetary policy doctrine. Classicism could eventually upset the existing boom by aggravating the current stage's weaknesses, namely slow money growth and income inequality. Policy should complement, not hinder, positive institutional change. Monetary policy should support bond prices by driving down interest rates and ending its incessant inflation fear and pronouncements. Business can assist the Fed by taking a pro-active approach towards controlling inflation. And this is something they can do, given that its business that administers prices and controls production capacity. More on controlling inflation in the next chapter.

Conclusion

The primary purpose of this book is to assess whether economic evolution is wholly or partly consistent with American values and principles. While this issue is fully addressed in chapter seven, a remark on money manager capitalism is now appropriate. This particular stage of finance has partially democratized the ownership of American business. Though effective popular control is not yet achieved, millions of people hold stock and bonds of the economy's most important enterprises. The middle class receives a larger fraction of their income from capitalist sources which supplements the wages and salaries earned by most workers. Accumulation of financial assets augments middle class security and retirement prospects. Long term, the trend in popular ownership of corporate assets is upward, and therefore, money manager capitalism ties an ever-larger percentage of Americans to the business interests of the country. This means that the interests of the public are more closely aligned with business interests, leading to a simultaneous decline in inherent conflictual relations over income distribution and an increase in democratic input into corporate governance.[16] While Classical monetary policy is not consistent with money manager capitalism, the latter is roughly compatible with basic American principles.

---

[16] Serious concern continues nevertheless for the economic welfare and political protection of millions of Americans who do not own mutual funds. Moreover, capitalism places a limit on the percentage of the population that can build wealth, for every dollar saved must have an offsetting debt somewhere else in the economy. Recall this discussion from chapters two and three.

While money manager capitalism is an increasingly important institution in modern life, bond and stock trading remain a potent force in financial markets. Trading alters financial asset values continuously. Speculation, practiced principally by wealthy Americans who own a substantial percentage of assets nationally, can potentially overwhelm the steadying effects of money manager capitalism. Therefore speculation is a threat to the current capitalist stage. Price volatility and sharp downward movements in financial market indices can undercut the benefits accruing to the economy from stable finance. Instability and asset-value depreciation may reverse recent trends in ownership and finance. Speculation is anti-populist.

Chapter 6

U.S. Monetary Policy

Monetary policy, conducted by the Federal Reserve and Treasury, has an important macroeconomic impact on financial stability and business vitality by affecting financing costs and profitability. It also affects income distribution. Monetary policy is largely understood as a policy that works through the banking system to affect the commercial and consumer sectors. Traditional commercial banking has been the key financial institution for funding business and creating money. But money manager capitalism is eclipsing traditional commercial banking as the leading financial institution and now Federal Reserve policy must be reexamined.

Central Bank Operations in the U.S.

The Federal Reserve is the central bank of the United States whose major responsibility is to set short-term interest rates by adjusting bank reserves. Banks maintain reserves or cash to assure sufficient liquidity to pay depositors who withdraw money, and to pay off checks presented for clearing. The process by which interest rates affect economic activity is called the monetary transmission mechanism. Changes in interest rates affect the amount of money in an economy and there is a somewhat complicated path by which central bank actions influence the system.

The single most important channel of central bank policy is the interest rate channel. The Fed., the nickname for the Federal Reserve Open Market Committee which sets policy, can inject reserves into or withdraw reserves from banks via the purchase and sale of government securities. Banks hold government securities and will sell them if the Fed offers a sufficiently high price or will buy securities if they are of a sufficiently low price. As reserves increase, the banking system becomes flush with money so banks tend to lower the interest rate they charge each other for loans. This rate is the Federal Funds rate. A contraction in reserves has the reverse effect. If the fed funds rate falls, other short and long term rates tend to follow in the same direction, encouraging firms and consumers to borrow and spend. Highly indebted people are likely to refinance their debts and the additional funds now available are often spent. An expansionary policy as this, if successful, leads to money creation as banks finance higher spending. Sellers of bonds realize capital gains as government bond prices increase, and the lower long-term borrowing costs for business encourages investment.[1]

Federal Reserve policy of affecting bank reserves has implications for the financial markets and economic performance. For instance, the first effect of a contractionary policy of higher interest rates is to raise the cost of funds to banks. Bank profits and bank stock prices decline. Bank profits fall despite a proportional increase in loan rates, because prior loans were made at lower rates but the current cost of funds is higher. Bank stock prices decline in response to lower earnings. Fewer loans and more costly credit result. Furthermore, higher rates paid by firms lowers their profits and may reduce investment if the rate hikes are large. Corporate stock prices fall as a consequence. And during booms when loan demand is surging, rising interest rates are inflationary as higher financing costs push prices.

Fed policy affects imports and exports as well by altering the exchange rate. The exchange rate mechanism works when interest rate changes drive up or down the value of the dollar on world markets. For example, higher interest rates encourage foreigners to buy American currency so they can purchase U.S. bonds or other interest earning assets. Higher demand for American money lifts the price of the currency relative to other currencies. American export businesses will find their sales dropping because their

---

[1] Bernanke and Blinder [1992] provide evidence that short run variations in the Federal Funds rate are attributable to policy decisions to adjust reserve supplies.

goods cost more to foreigners but U.S. consumers and firms increase their consumption of foreign products that are now less expensive.

Experience demonstrates that interest rate policy is an effective tool to alter business activity.[2] The low rates of the early and mid 1970s helped to maintain growth despite two oil embargoes. The high rates afterwards destabilized the economy and prompted a recession, and in the late 1980s contributed to increased debt loads and a fragile financial structure that led again to recession. Four years of falling rates assisted in reinvigorating the economy from sluggish early 1990s' performance and provided liquidity in the late 1990s to forestall any negative affects on the U.S. economy from world financial instabilities.[3]

The American central bank however is not always the engine that drives interest rates and borrowing. Bond traders, bankers, and Wall Street have their own opinions on interest rate levels, how robust to permit the economy to be, and the value of the dollar. Those who earn interest income desire higher rates as economic activity boosts profits and wages. Financial markets drive up rates over the course of economic expansion to enlarge the share of income going to financial interests. Financial markets also direct Fed policy buy moving bond rates up or down; strong economic growth or inflation will cause traders to drive up interest rates, signaling the Fed to follow course with higher short-term rates.

While the Central Bank affects the economy via interest rates, their policy is commonly known as "monetary policy", implying Fed influence over the economy's money supply. Traditionally, money growth was thought to be the all-important economic variable to control. Too much money growth fosters inflation, and inefficiently alters firm's investment decisions by creating confusion as to what endeavor or industry is profitable. Too little money growth creates a sluggish or recessionary economy. In actuality, the

---

[2] Because loan demand is insensitive to rate changes, the monetary authority must move interest rates substantially up or down to have much consequence on the economy.

[3] The world economy was struck with successive financial crises, beginning with the Mexican peso devaluation in the mid 1990s, to the East Asian currency crises, followed by economic difficulties in Russia and Brazil in the late 1990s.

central bank does not directly control the supply of money, but policy authorities throughout American history have made great efforts to limit money growth and maintain significantly positive interest rates through central bank actions. Such efforts contributed to occasional economic distress and a skewing of income to creditors.

History of Monetary Policy

This section reviews the major efforts by policy authorities and the financial industry to maintain some scarcity in money. Inflation is viewed by the authorities as indication of monetary mismanagement and as deleterious to economic growth. The higher principle of controlling inflation for its supposed social welfare benefits covers up the specific economic interests of financial elites who benefit from zero inflation and deflation. Price increases erode the value of financial assets and high interest rates, used to limit money growth and inflation, provide income to those who hold money as property.

An early philosophical aversion to a plentiful money supply is found in the Federalist papers written to support the adoption of a new constitution to replace the Articles of Confederation. In Federalist 10, Madison argues the importance of republics over democracies. Republics can enlarge and refine the opinions of the general public. And large republics in particular are good because they can guard against the evil intentions of the few and prevent the majority from usurping the rights of minorities. A federation of states therefore possesses a central government capable of protecting society from individual states that may print paper currency or abolish debts, or redistribute property, or perform "any improper or wicked project". Article 1 of the constitution establishes a congress with certain powers, among them include the right to borrow money, to coin and regulate the value of money, and to punish counterfeiters.

Throughout the nineteenth century, the American economy operated on a bimetallic monetary standard. Either gold, or gold and silver, formed the monetary base. Precious metals circulated as money, supplemented by bank notes. Bank notes were created when state chartered banks granted loans, and banks were limited in note creation by the possibility that note holders would demand specie for the notes they held. The First and Second Banks of the United States sometimes submitted bank notes to state banks for redemption to limit their note issue. The demands of financing the Civil War prompted congress to set up the National Banking system, which allowed national banks to buy government bonds. However, national bank note issues were limited by their capital stocks. Here in lies the basic problem in nineteenth century America, namely that its money supply was strictly limited by the amount of specie in the economy. Precious metal supplies depended on discoveries and technology to extract metal from the earth. Gold and silver supplies had no relation to the needs of commerce. Spending and commerce were somewhat restricted by limits built into the banking system's capacity to create money at reasonable interest rates. The financial system could not supply an elastic currency to meet the needs of business or the seasonal demand for funds by farmers without substantial changes in interest rates. Bank reserves would tend to accumulate in large urban banks as well and when agricultural loan demand increased, higher borrowing costs undercut commercial urban expansion.

Paper currency called greenbacks circulated during and after the civil war. This paper currency expanded the money supply and financed the North's prosecution of the war. But these greenbacks were gradually withdrawn as the government committed itself to running budget surpluses and redeeming the outstanding paper currency. With the withdrawal of greenbacks, the economy was put onto a gold standard by the end of the 1870s. The contraction in currency contributed to a protracted depression in the mid 1870s, a recession in the mid 1880s, and another depression in the mid 1890s.

The dominant theory of the time, supported and propagated by the elite financial class, contended that the gold standard creates stability by ensuring the maintenance in the value of money. Money is property and excessive note issue creates inflation that diminishes money's value. Inflation is a form of taxation or confiscation. And in the nineteenth century view, money's value had to be based on something with intrinsic value, like gold or silver. Limitations in the monetary base necessarily would maintain stability in the value of money.

The nation adopted a central bank early in the twentieth century, but only after continuous financial and economic problems compelled action to reform. Periodic economic downturns, often precipitated by an inelastic currency supply, interest rate spikes, and bank runs, created hardships for business and agricultural interests. Prolonged difficulties in farming, exacerbated by debt burdens, prompted the Populist Party political challenge in the late 1800s. A financial panic in 1907 led to a commission to study banking reform. The Federal Reserve was eventually established in 1913 during the Progressive Era reforms.

Modern monetary theory argues for a lender of last resort function of the central bank. The Fed., as described above, can inject currency into and withdraw cash from banks to set interest rates and provide the banking and economic system with liquidity. Banks in financial distress can rely on Fed injections to meet deposit withdrawals. A more liquid banking system can supply illiquid firms and consumers with needed funds to make payments to creditors and forestall bankruptcy. Open market operations, where the Fed buys bonds, is used to drive rates down so that debt ridden companies can refinance and improve their balance sheets. The pre-Federal Reserve economy had no institution empowered to create an elastic currency or determine rate levels. This subjected the economy to more frequent and intense cycles in activity.

Early twentieth century Fed policy employed the discount rate, the rate charged to banks who borrow from the central bank. The discount rate was raised at various times to stem the outflow of gold. Higher rate policies contributed to recession in the early 1920s and worsened the depression of the 1930s. In the mid 1930s, the Federal Reserve raised bank reserve requirements out of fear that the expansion then occurring would generate inflation. The higher requirements led to recession in 1937 and 1938. Following this recession, the Fed adopted open market operations as its main policy instrument. By purchasing bonds in the open market, the central bank kept banks flush with reserves and bond prices high. The resulting low interest rates assisted in recovery from recession and financing of World War Two. Interest rates remained low because of Fed policy through the early 1950s.

By the time of the Korean War, monetary authorities became increasingly concerned with inflation. This prompted a reversion in policy to an emphasis on price stability. The Treasury-Fed Accord of 1951 resulted in the Treasury Department's acquiescence to pressures to limit money creation and maintain significantly positive interest rates. Interest rates were allowed to trend higher, and did so from the mid 1950s to the middle of the 1970s. Nevertheless, on balance throughout much of this period, the Fed pursued an expansionary policy by keeping banks liquid through open market operations. This policy supported the rising government expenditures of the time, and together these policies promoted growth and stability.

Fed policy definitively shifted to controlling money growth in the late 1970s. Interest rates increased greatly as the Fed tried to restrict money growth to combat inflation. Interest rates relative to inflation, called real interest rates, increased above historic averages. Real rates have remained somewhat high ever since, except for the four-year period from 1989 through 1993. The authorities pushed rates down to help revive a sluggish economy, but promptly raised rates after an economic recovery appeared to be sustainable.

The graph below shows how the real federal funds rate moves over the business cycle, with recession periods indicated by vertical bars. The Fed controls this rate. Note that the central bank raises interest rates faster than

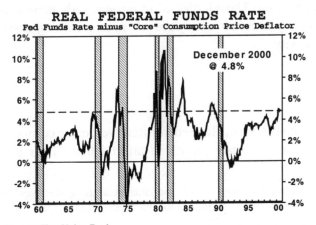

REAL FEDERAL FUNDS RATE
Fed Funds Rate minus "Core" Consumption Price Deflator

Source: First Union Bank

inflation during expansions and then must sharply reduce rates as recession or sluggishness ensues. The 1980s are somewhat of an exception, as collapsing oil prices first pushed up the real rate, followed by a sharp policy-induced fall later. The Fed returned to its highly pro-cyclical real interest policy in the late 1980s.

Economists and officials working for financial firms and the Fed are currently strongly encouraging the central bank to adopt a rule or an inflation target as policy.[4] Most rules stress the goal of price stability and bind decision-makers to follow the dictates of an equation-driven policy outcome. Officials are to adjust interest rates or the monetary base whenever some math model predicts inflation to rise. Inflation targeting permits greater flexibility than a rule but maintains emphasis on price stability by setting a policy goal of persistently very low inflation, whatever the cause of inflation. And most recently, central bank economists now want to model public policy after bank lending [Goodfriend 1999, 1–27]. Banks require collateral, monitor borrowers, set limits to borrower use of funds, etc. For-profit bank lending creates incentives for lenders to limit risk-taking on the part of borrowers, but lender of last resort lending has no such incentives; in fact, these economists believe that central bank practices promote or worsen financial crises by encouraging too much risk-taking. Therefore, they are now arguing that central bank lending become more selective and restrictive, even if doing so invites financial difficulties. The point here is to note the consistency in policy advocation. Though dressed in modern garb, these contemporary ideas steer policy to curtail money growth, raise borrowing costs, and deter economic activity.

Policy Reform

In the conventional view, the Federal Reserve conducts monetary policy whereby it controls money growth to affect interest rates and inflation.

---

[4] For a comprehensive discussion of rules and inflation targeting, see "New Challenges for Monetary Policy" published by the Federal Reserve Bank of Kansas City, 1999. For a further discussion on rules see Van Lear [2000].

Inflation is viewed as a monetary phenomenon. If the supply of money exceeds the demand for money, this "excess" liquidity is expended which drives up prices, regardless of the level of unemployment. The culprits are the government and/or central bank that allow excessive money growth. This story of the inflation generation process is incorrect because it assumes that the central bank can do more than it is capable of doing.

In contrast, heterodox economic theory argues that central banks are not capable of controlling bank reserves and the money supply; reserves are not a discretionary variable for Fed authorities. The supply of money is not a policy instrument because it is largely determined by the vigor of the economy. The greater the demand for bank loans by business and consumers, the more loans that are granted and the more new money produced. The Fed must supply cash to banks more or less on demand to maintain a smoothly functioning financial system. A growing economy requires money injection and this is accomplished by borrowers and lenders. Fed efforts to inject reserves into banks may not increase the money supply barring sufficient loan demand and efforts to drain reserves may fail as banks can obtain reserves from various sources [Wray, 1998, chap. 4–5].

Moreover, increases in the supply of money alone cannot raise prices. The initial affect of new money, by funding more demand for goods, is to boost sales and profits of business. Higher corporate income prompts firms to increase production, employment, and investment. Money growth and higher spending are essential if the economy is to grow. Business pricing on the other hand is conducted without regard per se for money growth. Pricing is an administrative decision made within the firm. Prices in most parts of the economy are set by company policy and are not determined in commodity or auction markets, nor in any direct way by the Federal Reserve. The inference here must be that the central bank cannot perform the function intended by many economists and government officials.

The implication of this is that inflation control should no longer be the responsibility of the central bank. Accountability for inflation should shift to the business sector who can provide a solution to inflation if indeed it is deemed a problem. Some studies, as cited by Thurow [1984] and May and Grant [1991], find that moderate inflation does not create serious macroeconomic problems. There is no empirical evidence that modest rates of inflation hurt growth [Thurow 1996, p187]. Government and economists should educate the public about the relative benignness of inflation and encourage business plant expansion when capacity constraints prompt firms to augment prices. In fact, price increases help business finance the plant expansion that later moderates the inflation.[5]

During expansions, business can moderate inflation by enlarging production capacity, by raising capacity utilization (ie, increasing output), or by investing in productivity improving technology. Vigorous economic expansions are accompanied by improvements in productivity [Business Week 2000, p33]. This tends to limit price hikes when demand is strong because unit costs fall or increase only a little [Eisner 1996, p32–36]. Action by business taken voluntarily or in response to profit incentive stemming from higher prices, or action that is in acquiescence to public policy inducement, will realistically come about if business regards its inaction towards inflation as limiting profits and growth. Without a pro-active move by firms to curtail inflation, the central bank will force inflation down by contracting the economy. Inflation induced from markup-financed investment is acceptable in that it promotes employment and growth. A booming economy drives up wages and shifts income distribution in favor of labor. Why invoke restrictive monetary policy, or let capacity constraints ration demand, prior to achieving full employment?

What if inflation arises from substantial cost-push pressures, such as in the 1970s, as opposed to a demand invigorated inflation? Traditional policy tools are inadequate in this case. Traditional tools only affect aggregate demand and therefore cannot directly lower prices except first by undermining profits and job security. This kind of inflation can be allowed to run its course through the economy. Or alternatively, some economists advocate incomes and buffer stock policies. The former policy attempts to control inflation by compelling firms and workers to raise their incomes no faster than productivity. Tax incentives can be employed to prompt compliant behavior. Government can also build buffer stocks of critical raw materials

---

[5] It seems far more sensible and humane to allow inflation to vary cyclically than employment.

and draw down on these supplies when commodity price inflation afflicts the economy.[6]

A complication to the inflation issue is the structure of the central bank itself. James Galbraith [1996] argues that the Fed is undemocratic and unconstitutional. The policymaking committee of the Fed is composed of 12 people, five of whom are representatives of the commercial banking industry. These members are not appointed by the President or confirmed by the Senate. Fed deliberations are not open to the public and there is no effective influence on the part of the public or its elected representatives over monetary policy. The central bank is by tradition and law independent of the political process. Further, these members bring a significantly conservative, Classical bias to policy formulation.

Federal Reserve policy as practiced is to offset Treasury deficit spending to maintain significantly positive interest rates. When the government spends, it injects new money into the economy and when it taxes, it withdraws money. Since deficit spending is the norm in modern times, the state usually increases the money supply available to the public. To limit the increase of money, the Treasury periodically borrows funds, thus withdrawing more money. Because injections do not correspond perfectly to withdraws, and the government typically runs deficits, money balances build up in banks and elsewhere in the economy. And here is where the Fed's main function lies. It conducts open market operations to reduce the cash available in banks and in the economy.[7] Or to produce a similar effect, the central bank limits its purchases of government bonds directly from the Treasury, thereby imposing a constraint on state spending and money creation. This policy affects the liquidity of the economy and in effect, creates a modest scarcity of money. Positive interest rates are maintained in this way. Understanding central bank behavior from this perspective leads to the inference that rates

---

[6] See Davidson and Davidson [1996] for a detailed discussion of the causes of and cures for inflation.

[7] Randall Wray develops in detail a coherent and insightful discussion of monetary and fiscal policy in his text Understanding Modern Money, 1998. Also see Bell [2000] on whether government spending actually needs to be financed.

need not ever be high and that the Treasury could easily maintain low rates if the Fed were to end its restrictive policy. Noting that government data and private studies all confirm a significant concentration in financial wealth, high rates necessarily contribute to a much more unequal distribution of wealth and opportunity in America.

If inflation is not a monetary event but a business pricing and capacity issue, if the Fed cannot determine the money supply but only set interest rates, and if the Fed's membership composition is too insular, then the Fed's interest rate maintenance function is superfluous and undemocratic. That is, the central bank's pro-cyclical interest rate policy and its inclination towards high rates to stem inflation is unwarranted and anti-social. Since the Treasury can affect the amount of money in the economy and the banking system via its spending and borrowing authority, the Treasury alone should conduct monetary policy in a fashion to consistently maintain low and stable interest rates. The Fed's supervisory and regulatory functions could be collapsed into an enlarged Securities and Exchange Commission. The new SEC would be entirely dedicated to the monitoring of all financial institutions and would conduct extensive research on the economy. In addition to ending the redundancy of having a central bank and a Treasury, the class biases now a part of monetary policy would diminish, as the federal government is less beholden to private financial interests.[8]

Concluding Comments

The above argument, if implemented, would indeed create significant change in policy. Only the Treasury, not the Fed, would conduct monetary policy.

---

[8] Keynes called for the termination of the power of private finance capitalists to maintain the scarcity of money. He foresaw the state as a vehicle to enlarge the flow of savings at low interest rates to promote entrepreneurial investment. See Keynes [1964, chap. 24]. In my plan, a deficit spending Treasury augments communal savings with money creation to establish a sustained low interest rate environment. The government banking function of the central bank is no longer positioned in an independent institution but folded into the Treasury itself. The Treasury therefore becomes the lender of last resort for the banking industry and private sector payments to the Treasury flow directly to the Treasury, not to a bank account maintained at the Fed.

Business, not the Fed, would be responsible for suppressing inflation. There is a disconcerting implication to this new arrangement however. A high employment, more robust economy is likely. But the very success of this strategy may also facilitate an investment-induced economic boom and destabilization, given business' bent towards investment, growth, and profits. Competitive pressures, profit expectations, and euphoria can lead to overproduction, excess capacity, and downward pressure on profit rates. A hedged positioned economy may become seriously speculative or ponzi, driving up interest rates and contracting profits, despite a low interest rate monetary policy. A sharp reversal in economic performance could result, destabilizing the economy. Despite low interest rates and ample liquidity, and the new policy outlook on inflation, such a scenario could produce a fragile financial structure and eventually recession.

Nevertheless, this new policy arrangement should help to stabilize economic activity by mitigating the disruptive effects of central bank driven monetary policy. Downturns initiated by collapses in business investment profitability remain possible however. And higher bond rates, driven by higher risk perceptions of lenders as firms and consumers increase their indebtedness during expansions, are not completely avoidable. Perhaps therefore traditional fiscal efforts of government deficit spending are sufficient to revive profits and the economy after a fall in the rate of profit. Government budget deficits and money manager capitalism work well in fostering investment and growth. Sustained cash flows and commitment to stock ownership can do much to achieve stable economic conditions.

The new policy arrangement is consistent with a money manager capitalist economy. A Treasury dedicated to low and stable interest rates and a business community committed to moderating inflation, provide support for bond prices. It also creates a better climate for growth since spending is facilitated. Financial institutional commitment of patient capital is encouraged since bond asset values are supported by policy, reinforcing money manager and mutual fund client commitment to stocks. And the policy would moderate income inequality by lowering the interest rate returns of the wealthy and by keeping the economy near full employment.

Epilogue on Inequality and the Fed

Stratified societies have existed throughout time and the United States is no different. Inequality in income and opportunity stem from substantial stratification in property ownership. Money is regarded as property and is used to generate income through the control of enterprise and through finance. High income is manifested in high money flows and substantial net worth. Federal Reserve conduct limits the money supply, placing limits on the amount of this property in existence and hence limits on the numbers of persons who can buy much and control resources and people. Current property distribution favors the few and the Fed maintains this status quo via monetary control. Limits to the money supply are not only consistent with stratification but reinforce stratification.[9]

---

[9] While much credit is available to the general public, this money is largely spent on consumer goods, which in turn simply perpetuates the current inequality in economic relations.

Chapter 7

Foundational American Principles

The United States since its inception is predicated on liberty, representative democracy, private property, and free enterprise. Liberty allows individuals to live and develop themselves along the lines they wish and permits diversity within society. The American notion of liberty creates a particular understanding of equality. Equality has an economic and political connotation. It means access to economic opportunity and property, and it also entails influence in government and politics. This understanding of equality is consistent with liberty and in fact is essential for liberty. The purpose of a representative democracy is to distribute power broadly, enabling the citizenry to affect legislation and policy. The people's interests and concerns have a bearing on political discourse and elected officials represent the various and competitive interests of society. Government power is limited through checks and balances. Private property provides some measure of economic security and independence from coercion. Economic power and initiative reside with individuals and their enterprises. A society committed to commerce and industry creates a dynamic system and promotes material prosperity. A unified and growing economy enhances productivity and hence living standards. Class distinctions arise from achievement in free enterprise and open competition, but such divisions fail to create a permanent and dominant hierarchy in any meaningful way. While Americans reject any policy to create perfect or near perfect economic outcomes, our notion of equality recognizes the dangers and drawbacks of distributional extremes.

These cornerstones of America make the nation distinct and are embodied in influential documents and reflected in defining eras and movements. This chapter takes a liberal interpretation of certain American core principles, and uses these principles as standards for evaluating current economic institutions.

Historic Roots of American Principles

Any forthright listing of underlying American values must admit that competing perspectives exist on the meaning of the American Revolution and U.S. history, and the nature of the Republic. While this text employs a liberal interpretation of what America means, an alternative view emphasizing the prominence of elites and their influence to set policy and guide events is a respected one. Without doubt, the leading figures of all eras had a disproportionate impact on their times and these people were often politicians and economic actors who commanded wealth and connections. But early American elites did break ranks from the European aristocracy. American political economy is distinguished by its liberal character, quite evident in comparison to much of Western history up through the eighteen hundreds. While elites had a profound influence in shaping America, they did so along lines more democratic and more economically free than other nations.[1]

Nor is it possible to show that all policies and practices were congruent with liberal American values. Slavery and racism prevented blacks from realizing any of the foundational values. The same can be said about U.S. policy towards the Indians, and when the federal government decided that Indians should be property owners, it was done by force. Discrimination against women and immigrants pervade our history. Various religious and utopian movements also existed in American history whose teachings and work stand at odds with the liberal values noted here. Even the prolonged

---

[1] Robert Bellah and his co-authors present what they believe are America's founding principles in *Habits of the Heart* [1985]. American cultural tradition is exemplified by biblical religion, republicanism, and individualism. These underlying principles animate the themes of justice, freedom, and success. Mores or "habits of the heart" involve ideas and practices demonstrated in religion, politics, and economics. Another effort to delineate American ideals comes from the work of Michael Lind [1995].

resistance to labor reforms and unions represents a certain departure from liberalism. Nevertheless, America stands out among the world's nations for its commitment to liberty, representation, property, and enterprise. These values are routinely practiced and preached. Therefore it is justifiable to argue that these notions define America and equally justifiable to critique policy and action that severely deviates from this framework.[2]

Having said this, the following provides an overview of the historical precedents that substantiate a liberal interpretation of America's meaning.

John Locke

Locke was an English political philosopher whose writings contributed to parliamentary democracy in England and influenced America's Founding Fathers in their separation from England and construction of the Constitution. In his Second Treatise of Government, Locke raises the issue of private property. Locke believed that God had given the world to men in common and to make use of the world to their best advantage. Locke argued that people have a property interest in their own body and that one's labor creates private property. And this property is both property in use and in title. People have a right to all of the property derived from their labor and have no temptation to acquire more property than they can make use of. If however property was accumulated beyond use or to the harm of others, the law was the means to limit or regulate how much property anyone person could acquire.

To secure and enjoy their properties, people formulate among themselves a contract as the basis for government. Majority rule prevails, and government makes laws to secure property rights. The force of community is used to uphold the law and promote the public good. The best way to secure property rights is with representative government, as this form of government avoids both anarchy and tyranny.

---

[2] Much thanks goes to political science professor Michael Tager for stressing the importance of debate over American values and inconsistencies that exist in America adhering to its stated values.

Declaration of Independence

The Declaration of Independence upholds the right of people to sever political bonds and that all people have life, liberty, and the pursuit of happiness as unalienable rights. Governments are instituted and they derive their powers from the consent of the governed. The purpose of government is to "provide ... guards for their future security". Great Britain's king is criticized for dissolving legislative bodies and not seeking the consent of legislative bodies for his policies. "A prince, whose character is thus marked by every act which may define a tyrant, is unfit to be the ruler of a free people".

The Constitution

The Constitution of the United States establishes in its preamble its various purposes, including the need to secure the blessings of liberty and its "We the people" that are responsible for the constitution. The general purpose of the constitution was to improve on the Articles of Confederation. One important weakness of the Articles is that they did not provide the basis for economic development of the whole nation. Monetary and spending powers of the federal government were put forth in the 1789 constitution. But importantly, a legal framework is established to promote a commercial society. The constitution protects contractual obligations, promotes the development of western territories and foreign trade, and provides for a national defense. Uniform rules for bankruptcies, patents, and copyrights are established. Property is protected in the fifth and fourteenth amendments. And section 4 of article 4, the federal government "shall guarantee to every state ... a republican form of government". Alexander Hamilton's "Report on Manufacturers" of 1791 followed the adoption of the Constitution and set forth a plan for industrial growth.

The Federalist Papers

This influential set of essays calls for a republican federal government, not a national government or pure democracy. It advocates a proper balancing of powers among government branches and between the states and federal government. From Federalist 39, a republic is "a government which derives all its powers directly or indirectly from the ... body of the people, and is administered by persons holding their offices ..." It is essential that government be derived "from the great body of people, not from an inconsiderable proportion, or a favored class of it; ..." It goes on to say that "the will of the majority of the whole people of the United States would bind the minority, ..." Federalist 10 lays out the various advantages of a republic and importantly notes the dilemma of securing private rights against the danger of faction yet preserving the spirit of popular government. Federalist 10 also talks of government's role in protecting private property rights, which due to unequal distribution, creates conflicting class interests. Thus government's function includes the "regulation of various interests". A republic can "refine and enlarge" the public's views. Finally, the Federalist Papers argue for Union based on various commercial advantages.

Alexis De Tocqueville

Tocqueville was a French nobleman who visited the United States in the early 1830s. Tocqueville's perceptions and insights about American democracy, as expressed in his text *Democracy in America*, are noteworthy for descriptive and prophetic accuracy. This astute political scientist searched for the principles of democracy, and desired to understand its advantages and disadvantages. He saw America as more socially egalitarian and meritocratic, and more rights oriented than countries in Europe. He observed a penchant for commerce and a desire to create wealth. But he thought that opportunity would not give rise to stark inequality that breeds revolution. People would acquire property and seek order, not an overthrow of the system. The spirit of democracy would affect other aspects of life such as literature and religion. But Tocqueville did believe that majoritarian democracy can become intolerant and lead to tyranny. Tocqueville believed that wisdom would assure the maintenance of freedom and democracy in America.[3]

---

[3] See the abridged version of Tocqueville's book edited by Richard Heffner [1956].

Jeffersonian-Jacksonian Philosophy

Thomas Jefferson and Andrew Jackson represent an influential line of American thought, often labeled Republican or Democratic-Republican. This view stressed the importance of a wide and roughly equal distribution of property ownership. While suspicious of government, this thinking is also concerned with the concentration of private economic power. National government should dedicate itself to the principles of democracy and freedom, and these principles should form the context for industrial development [Heffner 1991]. This thinking emphasized the importance of democratic input to stem government power, but also understood society in class conflict terms. Advocates supported a market-based economy composed of farmers and artisans who controlled both property and their labor. The growth of private concentrations of wealth, embodied in early corporations, justified state regulatory intervention.[4]

The Civil War – Reconstruction Era

The northern states were driven to fight the civil war to preserve the union and extend their industrial society southward. Lincoln's Emancipation Proclamation broadened the argument for war by advancing the right of liberty to blacks. The North's victory destroyed the slave system, a system inconsistent with founding principles. The war effort was followed by three constitutional amendments that granted former slaves their independence, expanded the franchise, and extended political equality through the due process clause and the equal protection clause of the fourteenth amendment. Republican policy fostered banking, railroads, agriculture, and education.

Bryan's "Cross of Gold" Speech

At the Democrat convention of 1896, William Jennings Bryan's speech to the delegates was one of the most noteworthy in American history. Bryan

---

[4] See the definitive work on the Jacksonian democratic era by Schlesinger [1953] entitled The Age of Jackson.

spoke eloquently about democracy, workers, taxation, and monetary policy. His speech was an attack on the gold standard. He claimed that the definition of a businessman was too narrow in application and that people who worked for wages were business-persons who create wealth. The nation was in need of someone to stand against "organized wealth". The "right to coin and issue money", ... and the policy of money, is a function of government. On the subject of democracy and economics, Bryan criticized efforts to exclude the "humbler members of society" from the benefits of growth and government. The democratic idea is that the masses should prosper and this wealth "will find its way up" to the higher classes which depend on the larger public.

The Progressive Era

The Progressive Era furthers political liberty and equality by its promotion of the referendum, the initiative, and the primary. Progressive income and estate taxes are put in place. Corporate campaign contributions are banned, women receive the vote, and the seventeenth amendment provides for the direct election of the Senate. In this era, government's role is enlarged. The state acts both to promote business and also to stabilize the economy from the negative consequences of capitalism. Anti-trust legislation and policy is pursued. Some social concerns are addressed, but industry is seen as efficient and economically progressive. Reformers build support for private property and free enterprise via reform.

The New Deal

While New Deal policies and extensions are far too comprehensive to summarize here, this era recommitted society to its values through government activism. The New Deal accomplished three feats: Income inequalities were moderated through progressive taxes, social programs, and support for the labor movement, economic activity was revived via demand management that promoted business profits, and the disruptive effects of financial speculation were tempered by enhancing the political stature of business and labor relative to finance.

Foundational Economic Principles

The above account establishes the historical roots of the most basic principles that underlay the American economy. American history should be seen as a continuous process of assessing what the core principles mean and trying to fully implement these principles. All along the way, institutional changes have occurred in the economy, driven by technology, the profit motive, and legal developments. Despite periodic efforts to the contrary, policy and economic evolution have created a contemporary political economic order significantly divergent from its principles. The ideal of liberty is not sufficiently realized. The ideal of representative democracy is not fully operative. The notion of private property is perverted. Only the idea of free enterprise, as expressed by the modern corporate-industrial, money manager capitalism model, is completely followed and adhered to.

Will the United States' future be one where our society proceeds to fully realize the ideals set forth in our founding and throughout our experience? If so, policy and reform must be grounded firmly in the core values of liberty, democracy, property, and enterprise. The most comprehensive historical effort to direct the U.S. along the appropriate path was the populist insurgency of the late nineteenth century. This era is captured well by the historian Lawrence Goodwyn [1978], who gives a concise account of the agrarian and worker revolt against the Guilded Age.

The Reconstruction and post-Reconstruction period produced a conservative, business dominated two-party system. While essentially practicing a laissez-faire public policy, government efforts were directed at promoting western expansion and industrialization. But most importantly, monetary policy was directed at paying down war debt, contracting paper currency, and reinstitution of the gold standard. Basing the money supply on the quantity of gold did not create a financial system that could consistently produce sufficient currency to meet the needs of commerce. The money supply was inflexible and relatively costly to borrowers. No institution existed, such as a central bank, to act as a provider of liquidity in periods of economic distress. These financial rigidities contributed to episodic recessions and financial panics, most injurious to debtors and workers. For much of the last three decades of the nineteenth century, the general price level fell, increasing real debt burdens and decreasing farm incomes.

In reaction to conservative monetary policy and economic instability, farmers formed the Farmers' Alliance to educate and organize Americans. Efforts were undertaken to create a farmer-labor coalition to push for populist and democratic political-economic reform. Specific demands were ultimately enunciated in the Omaha Platform of 1892. Populist planks called for agricultural assistance, labor and industrial reforms, political reforms, and government regulation or ownership of transportation and communication industries. Financial reform was centered on a federally administered national banking system, currency expansion, and a flexible currency system.

Populism fits well into the American tradition. Despite accusations to the contrary in the 1890s and after, populism is American to the core. Populism believed in sustaining individual liberty. It called for a genuine independence rooted in a fairer economy that allowed the majority of people to succeed. It wanted the economic security for all people that comes from property ownership and control over one's economic destiny. Populism opposed the social hierarchy and power inequality of the day, and advocated policies to support the producer-debtors that were most responsible for wealth creation. It advocated a real democratic order for the nation, based on legitimate political competition between viable parties that offered distinctly coherent alternative visions for the United States. Populism was committed to predicating politics on actual economic divisions, not racial and religious lines. A sustainable, mass democratic insurgency was necessary to overcome the cultural pressures to accept orthodox beliefs and act deferentially to elites. It believed in as well private property rights and enterprise, but in a system without privilege and where ownership arises from work and use of property.

America's foundational principles are set forth in important historical documents such as the constitution. In specific periods of history, like the Jacksonian era and the New Deal, these principles are affirmed and put into practice. And these same principles are expressed in Tocqueville's work "Democracy in America". Where might a recommitment by America to its core principles lead in modern times? What specific economic reforms are necessary to achieve an America true to its ideals? Had the nineteenth century populist movement succeeded in revamping the U.S., in what ways would our society be different today?

The Corporation

The dominant business of today is the mega-transnational corporation. The corporate form of business has proven to be the best device yet to accumulate wealth and power. No stockholder liability with regards to company actions increases the available financial capital to the firm and at relatively low cost. Stock exchanges enhance liquidity and offer diversification. This increases the flow of cash at reasonable expense to firms. Perpetual existence beyond the lives of executives or stockholders creates an independence of the firm from a given set of individuals. And the law sees corporations as artificial persons, providing them with all the protections granted to people yet with the means to acquire property and influence well beyond what individuals can accomplish. Corporations are protected by the due process clause, equal protection clause, and the contract clause of the constitution.

Because the corporate form of business is separate and distinct from its owners, the controllers can use the corporation to make their incomes far greater than what could be achieved from individual productivity. And because the owners and in most cases the executives are not personally responsible for the firm's conduct, corporate controllers are sometimes willing to use the corporation in anti-social ways. Consolidation is encouraged as a means to foster faster growth for the controllers. Firms can agglomerate property and people through tax-free exchanges of stock. These "stock swaps" allow the acquiring company to offer its stock for the target company, and no cash must be raised to finance the deal. Governments have attempted to force accountability onto firms through regulation, and have done so with some success. But capital mobility and the transnational dimension to large firms provide avenues to evade government restrictions. Economic dependency of much of the world on the leading 5000 corporations shifts much political-economic power towards the companies.[5]

The corporate elite represent an integrated and class-conscience whole [Domhoff 1983]. Substantial financial, social, and political links among corporate controllers foster communication and permit concerted group action to enhance business interests. Interlocking directorates, lobby groups, trade associations, business journalism, business advocacy organizations such as the Chamber, and corporate think tanks work together to promote not just specific firm interests. A larger corporate need for persistently supportive public policy and public sentiment is sought. Furthermore, people who run enterprises assess the political-economic environment, and discuss and develop plans to grow their firms. Strategic efforts are made to influence or initiate legislation, develop business and trade deals, and acquire financing. Board members and executives determine production capacity and capacity utilization rates, pricing, R&D spending, and product development. Actions as these are to raise market share, profits, and stock prices. Business competition and success require the demise or absorption of some firms, with industry consolidation the ultimate objective. The point is that corporate objectives are pursued by a class of like-minded people who have the same economic interests. These giant enterprises simply don't stand idly by being buffeted by market forces, but take direct action to affect their environment.

The large enterprise, apparently with no upper limit to size, has certain advantages. Some growth in size allows firms to exploit economies of scale. Large firms which produce more than small firms can spread increasing amounts of output over a given investment in capital, lowering average costs of operations. Certain technologies are more efficient when employed by large companies. And big firms' access to capital permits large-scale investments and risks taken on that may be prohibitive to small firms. Moreover, corporate and public interests are at times unified. Economic growth and growth in business size occurs concurrently with employment

---

[5] For coverage of business law matters, see Barnes et. al [1987], and for a critical view of corporate power bestowed by the legal system, see the publications of the Program On Corporations, Law, and Democracy at www.poclad.org.

and income expansion. Business induced technological change creates a vast array of useful and interesting consumer goods.

The corporate type of business has no particular or unique direct effect on the business cycle. But since the corporate sector dominates the economy, where corporations account for the bulk of sales, assets, profits, and investment, corporate performance markedly impacts the economic health of the remainder of the economy. Big business borrowing influences profits in finance and corporate investment drives the earnings of small company suppliers. Corporate dominated industries tend to be oligopolistic and price stability prevails over market determined prices. Therefore, shifts in demand more significantly affect output and employment, intensifying business cycle swings. To the extent corporations enhance inequality, cycles are further effected.

Despite certain advantages, the corporate form of business is found wanting on important grounds. For instance, the big firm is not consistent with liberty. Large corporations have come to control ever larger amounts of capital, workers, and communities. Their investment and production decisions have national and international economic repercussions. Money and its cost are under corporate control. The media industry, and hence its ability to inform opinion, is dominated by a few large conglomerates. Politics and campaigns are directed at achieving corporate business interests. Marketing and advertising influence consumer wants and attitudes. Freedom of expression is somewhat curtailed on the factory floor, and executives and supervisors determine the conditions under which people labor. Such economic prominence, garnered by about five percent of the population which owns and controls corporate business, limits true freedom. Liberty requires that people have discretion over more than which good or service to buy. It requires an autonomy where people can effectively influence their own economic destiny and political order.

A corollary is that reduced liberty, stemming from corporate economic control, must inevitably undercut representative democracy. Representatives become too beholding to business interests that finance campaigns or are themselves financially connected to an industry. As government officials, these individuals frequently work to promote those same interests, and state policy is circumscribed to the fostering of the prevailing goals of economic elites. Wealthy persons elected or appointed to public service will pursue policy informed by their own personal and class economic interests.[6] Public input is reduced to the ballot box where distinct political alternatives are compressed to people who advocate like policies that diverge only in degree. In fact, political dialogue tends to be restricted to certain options and issues. The economic inequality created by the corporation results in political inequality for society.

In what real sense are mega-corps privately owned? The law recognizes firms as privately owned when individuals, families or groups of people have equity at stake. Public ownership implies government ownership. But is it logical that multi-plant, multinational, multibillion dollar bureaucratic organizations are truly privately held or controlled operations? The dominant corporations in America have thousands to millions of shareowners, dozens of plants and suppliers, many creditors, and tens of thousands of employees. Their political and economic effects are pervasive and significant. Corporations account for the bulk of investment, R&D, profits, and sales in the economy. Though stockholders legally own these firms, real ownership is quite tenuous. After new cash is provided to the firm on the initial stock flotation, most shareowners trade their shares, so ownership moves from hand to hand. Speculation on the direction of stock prices occurs but there is little regard for ownership. No genuine commitment and close attachment to the enterprise prevails, only interest in financial speculation. Mega-corporations are therefore not meaningfully private in any sense, and are in fact publically owned and have substantial public force in society. Money manager capitalism has broadened the public nature of firms.

On a related point, profits create incentive for and provide reward to small business and entrepreneurial innovation. But in more bureaucratic operations, the role of profits is somewhat diminished; they lose their function as motivation and return to those engaged in entrepreneurialship. Profits

---

[6] It's inconceivable that the conduct of foreign policy or antitrust or environmental regulatory policy by corporate executives would mimic the policy constructed by people from non-corporate interest groups.

usually do not flow directly to people responsible for daily administration or production, or in any significant portion to employees in corporations.[7] While stock options are more important than in the past, most profit income is concentrated because of concentrated ownership. A portion of stock held is by shareowners that have not provided finance and hence do not own with commitment; they are mere appendages to corporations having purchased already outstanding shares through a stock exchange. This kind of ownership doesn't derive from finance and close association to enterprise, and the incessant stock trading carried on daily merely shifts the risk of ownership. Speculative stock ownership functions to provide outlets for wealth, not funding for enterprise; wealth producing engineers, production workers, and managers are non-profit wage earners. So profit is not the return to those running business organizations but partially functions as a pay-out to affluent non-workers who are not closely connected to the ongoing operations of the organization. Therefore, not only is big property not really private, it fails to channel profit income to those who run and develop the property.[8] And of course, diversion of profit to financial asset holders contributes to inequality since bond and stock ownership is concentrated.

Perhaps big firms are largely consistent with free enterprise. They are ideological supporters of free enterprise and often bring a competitive dynamism to economic life. Exceptions to the rule occur when barriers to entry preclude competition and ruthless business practices destroy what would otherwise be viable rivals. Galbraith [1979, 33–35] notes that the enemy of the small firm is highly visible, and in the form of advanced technology, specialization, and organization, that is, the large modern corporation. Only the large firm can afford the commitment of capital and time, and through planning, direct and influence the market. Small firms are thus usually unable to compete with large firms. To the extent that this characterization applies, bigness limits free enterprise.

---

[7] Executive incomes are so very high because profit is diverted as a supplement to their salaries.

[8] The controllers are responsible for reinvestment and hence have some control over the distribution of profit. To the extent that money manager capitalism is effective, profit as return to people closely responsible for the conduct of business is increasingly true.

Populist Reform Pressures

As a consequence of failing to sufficiently conform to American principles, the corporation should be reformed along populist economic lines. The large corporation, as other leading institutions, must comply with democratic principles. If the dominant business enterprise is incompatible with American ideals, it's likely that other institutions will fail in making the grade as well.

There is the potential for some reform pressure coming from the private sector. Money manager capitalism may be pushing the economy, to some extent, towards the democratization of finance and ownership. Money manager capitalism is about more middle class Americans contributing savings to the purchase of corporate equities and debt indirectly through mutual funds. Much of this money is committed for the long run and thus increases the connection people have with major firms. Instead of just an employee or consumer linkage, more have a financial stake in the continued performance of the economy's most significant enterprises. Corporate reputation and community involvement matter, for they affect consumer attitudes and stockholder interest. While most financial institutions retain voting privileges, institutional activism is surging [Blair 1995]. The 1990s brought increased attention by major shareowners to executive compensation, business restructuring, and corporate anti-takeover devices. Moreover, environmental, civil rights, and working conditions concerns are prominent in modern life, and get expressed via social funds which establish non-purely financial criteria for choosing which corporate assets to purchase. Activist money managers push for corporate responsibility resolutions at company meetings and in proxy statements. These factors have the potential to broaden corporate interests to a range of issues and to promote greater business civic responsibility.

Unions represent another democratizing force on the big firm; they always have. The issues of labor transcend narrow wage and hour concerns, though these two issues are of no small importance. A major effort is now underway to revitalize the union movement. Unions are moving southward and into the white-collar and professional ranks in organizing drives. This has effectively stopped the thirty-year decline in union representation. Corporate downsizings and restructurings to promote efficiency gains, and global investment directed at exporting white-collar jobs, create a somewhat analogous work experience among labor. Shared experiences and job insecurities promote interest in unionization across the labor force. Unions, strengthened by increased membership and financing, may once again act as countervailing power to corporate domination of the economy. Such success will push society to follow its democratic-populist economic roots.

The American political system has institutionalized representative democracy, however imperfectly practiced. There is therefore always potential for elections, and perhaps other means, to affect and promote the democratic impulse. Two applicable and influential theories of the state are the Galbraith-Heilbroner thesis and the Walker-Vatter thesis.

The Galbraith-Heilbroner thesis argues that the state and the corporate sector have been merging slowly throughout the twentieth century. This fusion is brought about by the problems and crises of capitalism. Economic intervention and business regulation by government is a necessity to maintain growth and social stability. By making the economy perform better, government enhances the support for the system while promoting business interests. Government intrusion into economic affairs comes at times with resistance and at other times by demand from corporate executives. Government spending assists corporate planning. This argument acknowledges the tremendous productivity and growth inclination of capitalism but also warns that a loss to liberty has occurred as society's beliefs are subordinated to business needs. The corporate-state fusion implies one of two possibilities. Either the democratic state will push the corporation towards the public interest, or the corporation will enlist the state in fostering commercial interests extensively and at the expense of social goals.[9]

The Walker-Vatter thesis argues that while continued relative growth in the size and functions of government are unlikely, absolute growth is a necessity. Continued government growth will be driven by periodic economic crises and humanitarian concerns for low income Americans. Modern economic development demands for infrastructure and environmental preservation are important factors as well. Interest group pressure and the

---

[9] The business-government fusion thesis is developed by Galbraith [1979] and Heilbroner [1976].

challenges of a high technology, global economy require a prominent government role in society. Importance of government is reflected in its spending and employment, but also by its large public administrative activities performed by regulatory bodies. Walker and Vatter concur with the above thesis that the state acts as a countervailing force to private economic power and simultaneously as a promoter of business.[10]

It is true that some convergence in the state and corporation has occurred. Government is inextricably linked to business, both as facilitator and regulator. This fusion, combined with the need for a vital state, does create tension over which goals, private or social, to pursue. The social democratic character of the state, demonstrated throughout American history, remains a potent force. Representative democracy remains institutionalized. Despite periods of inaction or regress, the United States government-corporate union will conceivably, by and large, pursue public service goals over the long run.

One final ally in promoting populism is the small business community. Small firms have values and political-economic interests in common with big business. This no one would deny. Nevertheless, small business operates under the constant threat of takeover by larger firms. They are frequently placed in unfair competitive arenas because big firms can exploit economies of scale and receive favorable discounts on merchandise from suppliers. The political power of corporations exceeds that of small enterprise. Transnational interests push for free trade and capital mobility, which together increase competition in domestic U.S. markets where small firms operate. Capital mobility at times means the allocation of local funds to finance national and international projects, and induces bank consolidation to meet the needs of multinationals. History has demonstrated that big business creates proletariats out of small business owners. Small business is critical of these advantages and privileges of size. And it is small business people that live most closely to the American ideals of liberty and free enterprise, honor self- and - representative government, and believe in the independence and opportunities offered by private property. Big firms violate these norms and small business may be a force for populist economic reform and revival.

---

[10] For a complete exposition of this thesis, see Walker and Vatter [1997].

Chapter 8

Conclusion

The effort undertaken in this book transits across a number of interrelated themes. We began by considering American income distribution. Income is heavily skewed towards a few due to the concentration of property, most notably facilitated by the business corporation. Great inequality fosters speculation and societal conflict, and can undermine economic growth. Democratic politics is undermined, and this inequality is defended by popular misconceptions of the Federal Reserve and business efficiency for example. Economic inequality becomes functional: Income disparities appear to be the logical outcome of a competitive, enterprising, and free society. Inequality is approvingly accepted as normative, undercutting the potential for popular critique.

The next section of the book discussed what factors play importance in economic growth and stability. The investment-finance link is central to understanding growth and why the economy moves through business cycles. Capital spending and its financing take place within the framework of both a corporate governance model and a particular economic environment. This framework, which evolves over time, influences economic performance. The economy moves through short and long run business cycles, and is affected by financial cycles. Growth requires net deficit spending and money creation. Ultimately, economic downturns are engendered by falling profits.

Stages of capitalist development are observed where distinct institutional features persist, but eventually institutions evolve and create a new stage. This book stresses the importance of institutional change in the way economic growth is promoted and financed. Governance of the corporation is the special institutional detail that informs and characterizes an economy, and defining periods are established by the particular governance system in place. The American economy has developed through a simple farming and handicraft system to industrial capitalism and finance capitalism. The twentieth century was markedly impacted by managerial capitalism, and now money manager capitalism characterizes the system. Each development stage has advantages and disadvantages for economic progress, and the current stage is seen as largely positive. Investment appears to be stabilized by finance and business ownership democratized by finance.

Monetary policy was the next focus of attention. Classical policy is in force presently, and a review of monetary policy history demonstrates that Classicism has usually been the guiding influence. U.S. policy has often displayed a strong dislike for inflation and strong support for limitations on money creation. Yet modern progressive understanding of money and policy stands in sharp contrast to and is critical of the conventional view and practice. The Central Bank cannot regulate the economy as Classical thought teaches, and their high interest rate policies have to do with undemocratic membership and class-biased philosophy of policymakers. The book proposes that the Federal Reserve be reformed and the responsibility for controlling inflation be shifted to business.[1]

The current practice of monetary policy is inconsistent with money manager capitalism, the newest economic era. Institutional evolution has, to some extent, reconnected savings with investment and ownership with control in corporate governance. Finance is now more supportive of stock prices, business investment, and consumer spending. While money manager capitalism is largely positive, it may at times promote economic stagnation by exacerbating inequality and limiting money growth.

The principal argument of this book was conveyed in the previous chapter. That argument states that American economic development has gone off-course, straying from its political-economic roots, with the rise of corporate enterprise. Specific principles were mentioned and their historical conditioning described. The corporate structure of business has gained too

---

[1] On both counts business should welcome such reform. Borrowing costs would be kept low and full authority over pricing would be granted to business.

much power by controlling too much property and too many people. The consolidation of productive enterprise by corporate business has created unjustified inequality. Private enterprise and property are perverted, representative democracy undermined, and liberty curtailed. The chapter concluded by identifying the forces at work that, over the long run, can push the corporation, and hence America's political economy, back towards its defining populist principles.

The remaining part of this chapter advocates particular progressive or populist reforms that may expedite a return to America's conservative underpinnings, and engages the reader in a discussion on American democracy. But first, a comment on the great economic expansions of recent history.

Elite Policy and Booms

With the hindsight of twenty years, we now know the fundamental causes of the economic expansions of the 1980s and 1990s. The 1980s expansion was driven by enlarged government budget deficits and falling interest rates. The deficits promoted private sector income and spending, and lower rates encouraged private sector borrowing. A second boom in the economy and financial markets followed the economic difficulties of the 1989–1993 period. Private sector deficits replaced government deficits as economic stimuli. More specifically, unprecedented household negative saving rates and borrowing propelled the 1990s expansion, with declining interest rates and refinancing giving a further boost to spending.

Both economic booms were aided by the stock market boom through the wealth effect, but the actual causal connection worked more the other way. The boom in spending and profit tended to justify increased stock values. But the boom in values could not have happened without a substantial shift towards unequal income distribution. Since most stocks are held by the top ten percent of income earners, their marked income increases in the last two decades financed unprecedented money flows into financial markets. And quite contrary to the interests of populist economics and progressive politics, the simultaneous occurrence of elite economic policies and rising inequality on the one hand and healthy job growth on the other has given the impression that these policies and inequality *caused* the job growth and general prosperity. While elite policies and income concentration had little to do with either of the past two economic expansions, the coincidence of events will undoubtedly cause some inertia in policy and belief, irrespective of future circumstances.

Short Run Policy Efforts

The preceding chapter outlined why the modern corporation is not solidly grounded in American principles, and what forces in the long run may create greater congruency with the principles. Over the short run, certain legislative efforts and policies could begin to pull America along a more populist economic path.

(1) Campaign Finance Reform: Genuine campaign finance reform is a must. Though direct corporate contributions to campaigns are prohibited, big money donations, called soft money, are channeled through the party system. Privately financed issue-advertisements supplement money contributions. The effect is to narrow the issues debated and limit party competition on economic matters. With much of the economy's wealth in corporate hands and individuals closely associated with big business, elite economic interests dominate campaigns and public policy. The current system has legalized corruption. Democracy is curtailed when the broader public input is limited or ignored. Economic interests do vary because people's functions in the economy, and way of earning income, differ. Sometimes labor and consumer interests are synonymous with corporate interests and sometimes they are not. Public financing and higher individual contribution limits, along with full disclosure of funding sources by candidates, would open opportunity for legislative pursuit of populist economic reforms.[2]

---

[2] An important impediment to rational reform is the Supreme Court's *Buckley (1976)* decision equating the free flow of money with free speech.

(2) Wealth Tax: A corollary economic policy is the wealth tax. Given the sharp increase in wealth concentration since the 1970s, elite economic interests have more clout in politics. Political parties have never been more dependent on financing, and competition among the wealthy to drive public policy continually raises the costs of campaigns. While campaign finance reform limits private contributions, the wealth tax curtails the concentration of sources of finance. The congress should finance public campaigns with public money from the wealth tax. Dugger [1990] proposes an eight percent tax on net worth above a personal deduction of $300,000 to be paid yearly. The current federal estate tax allows for a $675,000 exemption before a progressive tax rate structure goes into effect.

(3) Tax Progressivity: Any society following a populist agenda should put the primary burden of state financing costs on those who can most afford the costs and who need state programs the least. The U.S. must re-institute progressivity in the federal tax code by reducing payroll taxes on everyone and increasing income taxes on the top twenty percent of the population. This policy would bolster demand by increasing take-home pay of those inclined to spend, people who are relatively economically insecure, and by tapping into the savings of wealthier Americans to fund state-directed spending initiatives. With less of the economy's income lodged in upper-income brackets, less money is thereby available for Wall Street speculation, and instead allocated to enhance opportunities for lower income persons. Higher relative take-home pay for the middle class will further money manager capitalism's trend of democratizing ownership of big business.

(4) Mergers and Acquisitions: Another short-run effort should be to end mergers and acquisitions (M&A) among mid-size and large firms. M&A activity is primarily undertaken to agglomerate property and labor under the control of few people. Huge fortunes are possible only through business consolidation. In particular, the "stock swap" and "pooling of interests" accounting should be ended. The swap allows firms to pay for other businesses simply by exchanging stock that greatly reduces the cost of combination. Pooling permits acquiring firms to depreciate only tangible, and not intangible, assets gained from mergers. This accounting procedure increases reported

profits of the acquirer, thus encouraging stockholder support for mergers. Further, the burden of proving the worthiness of M&As should fall entirely on the corporate controllers who want to combine companies. They must demonstrate convincingly the technical necessity and/or economic efficiency of the combination. Importantly, the promoters of consolidation must also document how they intend to democratize ownership and control; what means will there be to broadly share decision-making and income? Otherwise, mergers above some asset level are ruled out pro forma.[3]

(5) Corporate Governance: Regardless of the adherence to populist reform, some big business combinations are likely to be permitted, and large corporations are the mainstays of our modern economy. Populist expression in these firms would come from societal pressures to create a stakeholder rather than merely a stockholder or executive governance system. Production, and hence economic value, by these firms is the result of the cooperative effort of all who labor in the firm. Therefore the rewards should be broadly distributed through ownership rights, giving all employees a claim to the residual of the firm. Margaret Blair [1995] of the Brookings Institution argues for a stakeholder capitalism that provides decision-making influence and residual claim rights to workers who possess firm specific skills. Such skills mean that labor's risk is not fully compensated for by wage payments. They bear firm or industry-specific-risk because their skills are not readily transferable across industries and occupations. Therefore, workers with firm specific risk have justifiable claim to the corporate residual. At the very least, Blair's limited stakeholder view should be adopted. This reform will enhance democracy in the firm and more equitably distribute economic wealth to those who are responsible for wealth creation.[4]

---

[3] The prevailing corporate position on mergers is that increasingly larger firms and ever greater industrial concentration promotes more competition, not less. This claim is enthusiastically made by the oil, airline, and multimedia companies in particular.

[4] Some companies offer employee stock ownership and profit sharing plans. Two noteworthy examples are United Airlines and Southwest Airlines.

(6) <u>Federal Reserve Reform</u>: Barring an outright overhaul of the central bank and a shift of monetary policy entirely to the Treasury, a short-run legislative effort to remake the membership of the FMOC is a possibility. The Congress would revisit the Federal Reserve Act and create a membership much more representative of the public interest. Unions, consumer groups, small business may prompt Federal action by filing suit in court to challenge the constitutionality of the Federal Reserve. Or the congress could mandate a low interest rate monetary policy, and one supportive of government deficit spending, in contrast to the current practice of high interest rates and a price stability mandate pushed by Classical economists.[5]

(7) <u>Fiscal Policy</u>: Alternatively, fiscal policy could be used to overwhelm the consequences of monetary policy. Bell [2000] shows that modern capitalist governments affect the money supply through fiscal policy and that central banking is about maintaining an interest rate target. Government spending adds to reserves and taxation drains reserves. In the *General Theory*, Keynes seeks a way in which to reduce the power of creditors to keep money scarce. In his concluding chapter on policy, Keynes argues that investment determines the level of savings and investment is enhanced from a low rate of interest. There is no intrinsic reason for the scarcity of capital that keeps interest rates up to a level that prohibits full employment. He states that "it will [still] be possible for communal savings through the agency of the state to be maintained at a level which will allow the growth of capital up to a point where it ceases to be scarce". Keynes argues for the state to affect the propensity to spend through taxation and fixing the rate of interest in order to affect the aggregate amount of economic activity [1964, 375–378]. The Treasury can accomplish this in effect by deficit spending. Deficit budgets would increase bank reserves and lower rates; the state would avoid the withdrawal of an equivalent amount of funds through bond sales. Of course for this to work with consistency requires a compliant Fed or a Fed whose attention is directed at matters other than bank reserves. This policy

---

[5] The Constitution already provides for congressional control of the nation's money.

arrangement is not now possible given central bank political independence, and its commitment to price stability and money scarcity.

(8) <u>Price Regulation</u>: In corporate capitalism, businesses are often price setters and consumers are usually price takers. Power and discretion lie with property owners, not buyers, in industries producing necessary goods and services. Therefore, populist governments must regulate price and profit of industries critical to economic infrastructure. These industries may include telecommunications, energy, health care, and transportation. A regulatory policy would include cost-based pricing and capacity regulation. Cost-based pricing keeps prices near average cost, thereby ensuring stable profit for industry reinvestment and reasonable charges to consumers. Capacity regulation is to ensure sufficient production ability so that industry can meet the public demand forthcoming from cost-based pricing. The larger purpose of regulation is to mitigate substantial income distribution shifts caused by price spikes arising from corporate market manipulation or shortages.[6]

Final Thoughts

Americans have always been proud of their democratic heritage. Elections and competitive campaigns are a routine part of life. Checks and balances

---

[6] Populists must combat the "market economy" theory espoused by Classical economists. In short, this theory says that markets direct resources and determine prices. Business and consumers react to market signals, and markets produce efficient outcomes. But the market economy theory is pure abstraction. The theory holds no person or private sector institution accountable for anything, nor does it permit the study of capitalism as a system; the theory reduces all economic activity to demand and supply interplay. Can we believe that an economy with multi-plant, multi-billion dollar enterprises, characterized by product and geographical diversification, amassing and employing huge amounts of resources, are not specifically responsible for economic development? Could these firms actually depend on unseen, impersonal, non-descript market forces for their guidance and profits? Or is it that market outcomes such as price and capacity *result* from industry decisions and behavior that inform traders when they buy and sell? Market prices are the consequence of industry-member businesses and speculators basing trades on the economic (demand and supply) facts of the industry, for which the industry in turn is responsible.

operate in government. Eternal optimism about progress abounds. A tendency exits therefore not to be vigilant in practicing democracy or assuring the sincerity and effectiveness of democratic institutions, especially those economic. But Americans must be careful not to confuse the forms of democracy with the facts of democracy. Indeed there are institutions of democracy in the United States, but the capability of these institutions in realizing democracy is hampered by the corporation and the Federal Reserve. In capitalist democracies, concentrations of power and the pressures of leading commercial interests pervert representative government. Real political democracy requires some quasi-egalitarian distribution of property and wealth; otherwise the bulk of the population has little input in and responsibility for social outcomes.

A progressive and populist political economy will rely heavily on public institutions. Public education, public task forces and regulatory bodies, public funding of research, etc., all are necessary infrastructure to a good society. Publicly financed institutions are responsible to the general public. Being publicly directed with public mandates assures a democratic mission grounded in social objectives and social welfare. These institutions are not beholden to any particular and narrow interest group, and therefore best promote an open, inclusive, and democratic order. Private institutions stand in some contrast. Some of these organizations are very dependent on a certain constituency for resources, marketing, and talent. This dependency gives these constituencies a dominant if not controlling influence. And since wealth and income are concentrated, any society that is extremely reliant on private financing and leadership will inevitably be guided by the dominant economic interests of that society.[7]

The dominant social force view of the state justifies public activism when it promotes property interests from the top down; otherwise strict limits are desired. Domestic supply-side policy directly boosts profits through favorable

---

[7] The tension between private and public institutions is illustrated well by the mid 1990s congressional debate over National Public Broadcast funding. Behind surface arguments was the more important issue of the degree to which commercial and conservative political influence should prevail.

business and upper class tax and deregulatory policies, and foreign policy works to open markets and subsidize investment. Denigration of state activism is reserved for social programs, business regulation, market manipulation, and any effort designed to direct resources from the bottom up. Conservatives, with patriotic zeal, are great advocates of the American state during war anniversaries and July 4th, and encourage adoption by other nations of the American system of government. Yet the same people go to great length to separate Americans from their government through condemnation and ridicule of socially predicated public sector initiatives. Any progress on populist economic policy requires an alternative notion of American limits and use of government. Use of government must be redefined to mean minimal state assistance to corporate interests and increased energy at promoting a wide distribution of property ownership, enterprise, and opportunity. The state more so than the modern corporation is open to democratic input and social concern, given elections, representation, and its public mandate.[8]

Often the American political center is regarded as a place of reason and compromise. Does American populism fit well into the political center? Does the Center reflect populist notions? The answer is an unequivocal "no". The Center in any political economy largely represents the ideas and interests of the dominant economic force. A vital Center can move legislation and in the case of the U.S., a corporate-Wall Street agenda can be advanced. While avowedly pro-growth, this agenda tends to undermine various social protections and to enhance income inequality. Democratic pressures may moderate such effects. But any sort of populist program will be off limits. Despite an historical association of populism to American principles, and an aversion of Center politics to extremis policies (as understood by the prevailing power structure), a populist program necessarily challenges the current drift in economic and political power.

American political economy consists of a philosophical conflict and competition among three positions. Conservatives are unrelenting advocates of free enterprise, private property, representative government, and freedom,

---

[8] Champlin and Knoedler [1999] document government efforts to redistribute resources to corporations through lax anti-trust enforcement and subsidies.

and economic freedom in particular. They support private sector outcomes and limited government. The American left or progressives are quite critical of capitalism for its unequal dispersion of wealth and concentrations of political-economic power in business and Wall Street. They advocate substantial government supervision and regulation of business, and public policies designed to mitigate large inequalities. Liberals form a middle ground. They are defenders of private property rights and liberty. They accept some inequality produced through competition and differences in skills. Active government is wanted to address various market failures and persistent poverty, and an energetic state is one that reflects democratic input. The Right, Left, and Middle struggle for the hearts and minds of the public.

What is evident is the basis for philosophical agreement among these contending groups. To be conservative means to be for America's founding principles because conservatism is about the promotion and protection of traditional and defining values. Reformers on the other hand foster, and are open to, change. They work to create change, and are not wholly comfortable with contemporary conditions or institutions. American reformers, with some exceptions, are avid democrats. They believe in civil liberties, elections, responsive and open government, and acknowledge the freedoms and opportunities rendered by private property. America's founding principles are in one sense conservative because they are foundational, but are simultaneously progressive because they represent such a sharp break with historical and current principles that inform other societies. Democracy and economic populism are consistent notions. They are insurgent to power hierarchies and elite interests. So therefore, at least philosophically, to be conservative is to act progressively; to be progressive or liberal is to think conservatively. Conservative principles are radically based and progressives apply conservative principles when advocating reform. Perhaps there is a basis for unity of thought and no warranted reason for much philosophical contention in America?[9]

---

[9] So therefore political division exists around means, not philosophical principles or ends. But conservatives must admit that their means of anti-government – economic libertarianism is responsible for the current corporate dominated perversion of American norms.

The philosophical division in the U.S. stems from Conservative misunderstanding of historical evolution and the Left's misunderstanding of how radically insurgent are America's basic principles. Conservatives do not see or knowingly refuse to acknowledge that institutional economic change since the 1770s, especially in the dominant business enterprise, has carried America away from its foundational principles. The Left does not see that our great reform eras and that noted liberal activists often employed the foundational principles to critique the political-economy and to create a reasoned basis for reform policies.

But more than misunderstanding prevails. Elite economic interests, vested in the maintenance and expansion of the corporate form of business, and in the continuance of Classical monetary policy, have successfully portrayed themselves as heirs and proselytizers of American values. And having long dominated the arena of debate and information, these interests successfully characterize reformers as anti-American or out of the mainstream.[10] The foundational principles are also used to justify the current economic structure and elite control of government. For example, Locke's understanding that property arises from labor is misapplied when used as a defense of corporate property rights. Workers for corporations do not ever own what they make and hence a portion of their labor is stolen from them. Moreover, with the end of the New Deal-Great Society era, neo-liberalism is about greater use of government to promote a global corporate world order. The consequence of all this is that economic policies espoused by the major parties are quite similar; positions of most candidates for office differ by degree and do not represent fundamental philosophical distinctions. What America has are competitive elections, over similar policies, between two corporate parties who have no effective outside competition. The electorate is effectively split, forced to accept either one of two corporate political platforms, and dissuaded from supporting populist politics.

Power distrusts democracy and dislikes populist economic policy. Momentum is now with the dominant corporate culture. Nevertheless,

---

[10] Progressive inclinations to employ government activism and market regulations appear to set them apart from American tradition and open reformers to criticism.

American loyalty to their core values and constitutional principles remains steadfast. In times of economic problems and crisis, leaders will look again to these principles for guidance. The United States will move back toward the path of economic populism. Crisis will reinvigorate a populist challenge to corporate capitalism.

The two major political parties deserve the parting comment. The parties have always been elitist parties evidenced in their leadership and financial base. At times, these parties take on populist overtones as crises and democratic pressures require reformist action. During some of the twentieth century, the Democrat Party has displayed populist tendencies and thus attracted many disgruntled voters. But with civil and women's rights largely addressed, environmental policy a mainstay of private and government efforts, and the economy stabilized via intervention, there are no current pressing issues necessitating either party to offer a substantive economic policy difference to the electorate. The move of Democrats to the political right in the 1980s and 1990s has progressed to the point where the parties have largely converged. Any further accommodation by the Democrats will undercut any purpose to maintaining two elite parties. American campaigns will lack real electoral competition and present no sharp programmatic contrast. If there is not formal party merger, one party will exit, or become a permanent minority, and it's likely to be the Democrats. If this occurs, a schism will develop between the practical corporate-driven political economy and the American political economic tradition: Policy won't be rooted in populist democratic philosophy. This will mark a national failure to abide by the core principles. Such a blatant incongruency may resuscitate a Populist Party challenge to single party domination.

Bibliography

Baran, Paul A. and Paul M. Sweezy. Monopoly Capital. New York: Monthly Review Press, 1966.

Barnes, James. Law for Business. Homewood: Irwin, 1987.

Bell, Stephanie. Do Taxes and Bonds Finance Government Spending? Journal of Economic Issues 34. September 2000, 603–617.

Bellah, Robert, Richard Madsen, William Sullivan, Ann Swidler, and Steven Tipton. Habits of the Heart. Berkeley: University of California Press, 1985.

Bernanke, Ben and Alan Blinder. "The Federal Funds Rate and the Channels of Monetary Transmission" American Economic Review. 82 September 1992, 901–921.

Berle, Adolph and Gardiner Means. The Modern Corporation and Private Property. New York: Commerce Clearing House, 1932.

Blair, Margaret. Ownership and Control. Washington: Brookings Institution, 1995.

Brown, Christopher. "Rise of the Institutional Equity Funds: Implications for Managerialism." Journal of Economic Issues 32, September 1998, 803–821.

Business Week. Various issues.

Canterbery, E. Ray. Wall Street Capitalism. New Jersey: World Scientific Publishing Co., 2000.

Champlin, Dell and Janet Knoedler. "Restructuring by Design: Government's Complicity in Corporate Restructuring." Journal of Economic Issues. 33, March 1999, 41–57.

Chandler, Alfred. The Visible Hand. Boston: Harvard University Press, 1977.

Coy, Peter. "A New Calculus For A New Economy." Business Week. November 8, 1999, 34–35.

Crotty, James R. "Owner-Manager Conflict and Financial Theories of Investment Instability: A Critical Assessment of Keynes, Tobin, and Minsky." Journal of Post-Keynesian Economics 12, Summer 1990A: 519–542.

Crotty, James R. "The Institutional Foundation of Keynes' Methodology." Journal of Economic Issues 24, September 1990B: 761–780.

D'Arista, Jane. Reforming International Financial Architecture. Challenge. May/June, 2000, 44–82.

Davidson, Paul. Post Keynesian Macroeconomic Theory. Cheltenham: Edward Elgar, 1994.

Davidson, Greg and Paul Davidson. Economics for a Civilized Economy. Armonk: M.E. Sharpe, 1996.

Domhoff, G. William. Who Rules America Now? New York: Simon and Schuster, 1983.

Drucker, Peter. Post-Capitalist Society. New York: Harper Business, 1993.

Drucker, Peter. Managing in a Time of Great Change. New York: Dutton-Truman Tally, 1995.

Drucker, Peter. Beyond the Information Revolution. Atlantic Monthly. October 1999, 47–57.

DuBoff, Richard. Accumulation and Power. Armonk: M.E. Sharpe, 1989.

Dugger, William. The Wealth Tax: A Policy Proposal. Journal of Economic Issues 24. March 1990, 133–144.

Dugger, William. The Great Retrenchment and the New Industrial State. Review of Social Economy. Spring 1993, 453–471.

Economic Report of the President. Council of Economic Advisors. Various issues.

Edwards, Franklin. The New Finance. Washington: AEI Press, 1996.

Eisner, Robert. "Deficits and Unemployment" published in Reclaiming Prosperity, Edited by Todd Schafer and Jeff Faux. Armonk: M.E. Sharpe, 1996.

Federal Reserve Bulletin. various issues.

Friedman, Milton. Free To Choose. New York: Harcourt Brace Jovanovich, 1980.

Fortune, Peter. "Mutual Funds, Part I: Reshaping the American Financial System." New England Economic Review. July/August 1997, 45–72.

Fortune, Peter. "Mutual Funds, Part II: Fund Flows and Security Returns." New England Economic Review. Jan./Feb. 1998, 3–22.

Foster, J. Fagg. The Reality of the Present and the Challenge of the Future. Journal of Economic Issues. December, 1981, 963–968.

Galbraith, James. "The Federal Reserve: Give It Till Sunset" published in Reclaiming Prosperity, edited by Todd Schafer and Jeff Faux. Armonk: M.E. Sharpe, 1996.

Galbraith, John K. The New Industrial State. Boston: Houghton Mifflin, 1979.

Glassman, James and Kevin Hassett. "Dow 36,000." The Atlantic Monthly. September 1999, 37–58.

Godley, Wynne. Seven Unsustainable Processes. Jerome Levy Economics Institute, 1999.

Godley, Wynne and Bill Martin. How negative can U.S. Saving Get? Policy Note. Jerome Levy Economics Institute, 1999/1.

Godley, Wynne and Randall Wray. Can Goldilocks Survive? Policy Note. Levy Economics Institute, 1999.

Goodfriend, M. Monetary Policy Comes of Age: A 20th Century Odyssey. Federal Reserve Bank of Richmond, Economic Quarterly, Winter 1997, 1–22.

Goodfriend, M. and Jeffrey Lacker. Limited Commitment and Central Bank Lending. Economic Quarterly. Federal Reserve Bank of Richmond, 85 Fall 1999, 1–27.

Goodwyn, Lawrence. The Populist Moment. Oxford: Oxford University Press, 1976.

Gordon, David. Up and Down the Long Roller Coaster. Printed in U.S. Capitalism in Crisis. Union for Radical Political Economics, 1978.

Gurley, J.G. and E.S. Shaw. Money in a Theory of Finance. Washington D.C.: Brookings Institution, 1960.

Heffner, Richard. A Documentary History of the United States. New York: Mentor, 1991.

Heilbroner, Robert. Business Civilization in Decline. New York: W.W. Norton, 1976.

Heilbroner, Robert. The Making of Economic Society. Englewood: Prentice-Hall, 1985.

Herman, Edward. Corporate Control, Corporate Power. Boston: Cambridge University Press, 1981.

Hetzel, R. A Quantity Theory Framework for Monetary Policy. Economic Quarterly. Federal Reserve Bank of Richmond, Summer 1993, 35–47.

Kalecki, Michal. Selected Essays on the Dynamics of the Capitalist Economy. Cambridge: Cambridge University Press, 1971.

Keynes, John M. The General Theory of Employment, Interest, and Money. New York: Harcourt Brace, 1964.

Kerbo, Harold. Social Stratification and Inequality. New York: McGraw-Hill, 1991.

Khan, Aubhik. The Finance and Growth Nexus. Business Review. Federal Reserve Bank of Philadelphia. January/February, 2000, 3–14.

Kopcke, Richard. "Profits and Stock Prices: The Importance of Being Earnest." New England Economic Review, March/April 1992: 27–44.

Lind, Michael. The Next American Nation. New York: The Free Press, 1995.

Maki, Dean and Michael Palumbo. Disentangling the Wealth Effect: A Cohort Analysis of Household Saving in the 1990s. Federal Reserve Bank Finance and Discussion Series, paper #21, April 2001.

May, Ann Marie and Randy Grant. Class Conflict, Corporate Power, and Macroeconomic Policy: The Impact of Inflation in the Postwar Period. Journal of Economic Issues. June 1991, 373–381.

Mayer, Martin. The Bankers. New York: Truman Talley Books, 1997.

McDermott, Karl A. "The Evolution of the Investment System: Keynes' Theory of Employment and Money Revisited." Review of Social Economy 51 Spring 1993: 62–85.

Means, Gardiner. The Corporate Revolution. G.C. Means Papers, Series I, FDR Library, 1933.

Minsky, Hyman. Stabilizing An Unstable Economy. New Haven: Yale University Press, 1986.

Minsky, Hyman. "Schumpeter: Finance and Evolution." in Evolving Technology and Market Structure, edited by Arnold Heertje and Mark Perlman. Ann Arbor: University of Michigan Press, 1990.

Mitchell, Lawrence. Stacked Deck. Philadelphia: Temple University Press, 1998.

Moore, Basil. "The Endogenous Money Supply." Journal of Post Keynesian Economics, 1988, 372–385.

Myers, Margaret. A Financial History of the United States. New York: Columbia University Press, 1970.

Nakamura, Leonard. "Intangibles: What Put the New In the New Economy?" Business   Review. Federal Reserve Bank of Philadelphia. July/August 1999, 3–16.

National Public Radio report. January 8, 1999.

New Challenges for Monetary Policy. A Symposium sponsored by the Federal Reserve Bank of Kansas City. August, 1999.

Palley, Thomas. "Contradictions Coming Home To Roost? Income Distribution and the Return of the Aggregate Demand Problem". Working Paper 332, Levy Economics Institute, July 2001, 1–16.

Parker, Edgar and Phillip Parker. "Venture Capital Investment: Emerging Force in the Southeast." *Economic Review*, Federal Reserve Bank of Atlanta. Fourth Quarter, 1998, 36–47.

Program on Corporations, Law, and Democracy. "By What Authority" Various issues. www.proclad.org.

Puth, Robert. American Economic History. Chicago: Dryden Press, 1982.

Randall, Richard. Safeguarding the Banking System in an Environment of Financial Cycles. Federal Reserve Bank of Boston, 1993.

Reich, Robert. The Work of Nations. New York: Vintage Books, 1992.

Schumpeter, Joseph. Capitalism, Socialism, and Democracy. New York: Harper and Row, 1942.

Selections from The Federalist: Hamilton, Madison, Jay. Edited by Henry Commager. Arlington Heights: Harlan Davidson, 1949.

Sherman, Howard. The Business Cycle. Princeton: Princeton University Press, 1991.

Schlesinger Jr., Arthur. The Age of Jackson. Boston: Little, Brown and Co., 1953.

Survey of Current Business. various issues.

Szatmary, David. Shays' Rebellion. Boston: University of Massachusetts Press, 1980.

Thurow, Lester. Dangerous Currents. New York: Vintage Books, 1984.

Thurow, Lester. The Zero-Sum Solution. New York: Simon and Schuster, 1985.

Thurow, Lester. Head To Head. New York: Warner Books, 1992.

Thurow, Lester. The Future of Capitalism. New York: Penguin, 1996.

Tocqueville, Alexis. Democracy in America. Edited by Richard Heffner. New York: Mentor, 1956.

U.S. News and World Report. Various issues.

Useem, Michael. Investor Capitalism. New York: Basic Books, 1996.

Van Lear, William. A Review of the Rules Versus Discretion Debate in Monetary Policy. Eastern Economic Journal 26. Winter 2000, 29–40.

Walker, John and Harold Vatter. The Rise of Big Government in the United States. Armonk: M.E. Sharpe, 1997.

Wall Street Journal. various issues.

Wall Street Week program. PBS. August 6, 1999.

Weber, Max. The Protestant Ethic and the Spirit of Capitalism. London: Routledge, 1992.

Whalen, Charles. Money Manager Capitalism and the End of Shared Prosperity. Journal of Economic Issues. 31, June 1997, 517–525.

Whalen, Charles. Hyman Minsky's Theory of Capitalist Development. A paper delivered at the Levy Economics Institute, April 21, 1999.

Wolfson, M. Financial Crises. Armonk: ME Sharpe, 1986.

Wolfson, Nicholas. The Modern Corporation. New York: The Free Press, 1984.

Wolman, William and Anne Colamosca. The Judas Economy. Boston: Addison-Wesley, 1997.

Wray, L.R. Understanding Modern Money. Cheltenham: Edward Elgar, 1998.

Index